# GHOSTS & GRAVESTONES of York

# GHOSTS & GRAVESTONES of York

PHILIP LISTER

First published in 2007 by Tempus Publishing

Reprinted in 2009 by
The History Press
The Mill, Brimscombe Port,
Stroud, Gloucestershire, GL5 2QG
www.thehistorypress.co.uk

Reprinted 2010, 2012, 2013



British Library Cataloguing in Publication Data.
A catalogue record for this book is available from the British Library.

ISBN 978 0 7524 4357 7

Typesetting and origination by
Tempus Publishing Limited.
Printed in Great Britain.

# Contents

# Acknowledgements

I was most flattered when I was first approached by Tempus Publishing some time during 2005 to write a book on the *Ghosts & Gravestones of Haworth*, and though I like to believe that I have a fairly busy life, the project began.

With some trepidation the official launch took place at the Brontë Parsonage Museum in Haworth in June 2006, and to my amazement the reviews were great, and within four weeks the sales were so good that the book went for its first reprint. By the end of the year the book went for its second reprint, and somehow I had agreed to produce a second book, *Ghosts & Gravestones of York*.

So once again I find myself adding my acknowledgements – to my beloved partner Jenny, who continues to share my dreams, and whose sense of humour, love of life and common sense still remain a constant inspiration to me. To David Buxton, Cate Ludlow and everyone at Tempus Publishing, for all their help and encouragement in producing this book. To Bernard Nicholson, my most helpful York taxi driver for all his help with the location photography.

And finally dear reader, to you, for taking the time to read my stories – thank you.

# Bibliography

Bland, James, *The Common Hangman*
Booth, R.K., *York: The History and Heritage of a City*
Dickens, Charles *All Year Round*
Defoe, Daniel, *A Tour Through the Whole Islands of Britain*
Hall, Richard, *York (English Heritage)*
Henson, Keith, *Foul Deeds & Suspicious Deaths in York*
Jones, Mark W., *The Complete Snickelways of York*
Mathews, Rupert, *Haunted York*
Mitchell, John V., *Ghosts of an Ancient City*
Murray, Hugh, *This Garden of Death: The York Graveyard Guide*
Roberts, Andy, *Ghosts and Legends of Yorkshire*
Rowntree, S., *Poverty: A Study of Town Life*
Yorkwalk

# Chapter 1
# A Brief History of the City

*Quote from a King*

King George VI once famously observed that 'the history of York was the history of England', and the city has most certainly played a leading role in the country's military, religious and commercial development for almost 2,000 years.

First the Romans made it their major northern garrison and named it *Eboracum*, when in AD 71 the legendary 9th Legion was ordered to march north from its Lincoln stronghold and subdue the hostile northern tribes, which were threatening the Roman advance. A fortress was established and this developed into a sophisticated centre of government and commerce, as well as a military headquarters. In fact, Roman York evolved in a way unique in Roman Britain at the time. Facing each other across the Ouse were a great military centre and a great civilian centre – a thriving, cosmopolitan place, which enjoyed a Mediterranean lifestyle. It was ideally placed to defend this part of their empire against the warring northern tribes. York's essential city layout is still Roman. The two key streets in the ancient city, the *Via Praetoria* and *Via Principalis*, later became known as Stonegate and Petergate, and to this day they still run along the same routes as they did two millennia ago.

*First Christian Emperor*

Further reminders of the Imperial Age are the Roman columns in Deangate, recovered from the foundations of the Minster and all that survives of what was once a massive military nerve-centre; the remnants of a bath-house in the Roman Baths public house in St Samson's Square and perhaps most impressive of all, the Multangular Tower, dating from first-century Eboracum and part of the legionary fortress. Here the chisel marks of Roman stonemasons can still be clearly seen. In 306, Constantine the Great was crowned Roman Emperor in York, probably on the site which is now York Minster. A statue now stands in front of the Minster to commemorate the event; Constantine was to become the first Emperor to embrace Christianity. Yet just over one hundred years later the Romans abandoned Eboracum and the rest of Britain.

*Saxon York*

The tribes they had been drafted in to keep out overran the city, and the so-called Dark Ages of the Saxon rule began. There followed a time of destruction and strife about which little is known. Legend claims King Arthur captured the city at one time during this period. In the seventh century the Saxons settled within the fortress walls, and in 627 Paulinus baptised King Edwin of Northumbria into Christianity. The small wooden church built on the site was the predecessor of the Minster. In the eighth century, a grammar school was founded, and students attended from all over Europe, to study under the great teacher, Alcuin. St Peter's School, now in Clifton, claims direct descent from it. When the Vikings conquered the city they would find the locals still living in the 800-year-old ruins of a once great European city!

*A thriving, cosmopolitan place, which enjoyed a Mediterranean lifestyle.*

*The Long Ships Arrive*

Of the many extraordinary chapters in York's history, possibly the one which most captures the public imagination is that period of less than one hundred years towards the end of the first millennium AD when the Saxon settlement of Eorforwick became Jorvik and the city found itself under Viking rule. In 866 the Viking 'Great Army', a huge armada of Danish pirates, sailed up the Ouse and seized Eorforwick under the leadership of the memorably named Ivar the Boneless. The following year they made York their capital. The conquest lasted until 954 when the last Viking ruler, the equally colourfully monikered Eric Bloodaxe, the deposed King of Norway, was driven out by the English King Eadred. During their time in York the Vikings had doubled the size of the town and turned it into one of the greatest trading ports in the whole of Northern Europe: they established a thriving and prosperous seaport with trading links as far east as the Baltic coast of Russia, stretching westward to Greenland.

*Mysterious Warriors*

One of the reasons why the Scandinavian invaders still exercise such a hold on the imagination is that apart from the unique community uncovered in Coppergate around thirty years ago, little evidence remains of their British reign. There is something mysterious and contradictory about these warriors who despite their fearsome warlike image and track record as pillagers were in fact sophisticated traders. Even their reputation as heathens is inaccurate: Danish Vikings in York adopted Christianity and worked with the Church.

*In the gardens of the Yorkshire Museum lie the thirteenth-century ruins of St Mary's Abbey.*

*The Second City of England*

In 1066, King Harold of England was to defeat his brother Tostig and King Hardrada of Norway at Stamford Bridge – just six miles from York – prior to marching southwards to defeat at the hand of William the Conqueror. The victor, William, came to York to subdue rebellion in the troublesome north which he achieved by a scorched-earth policy, causing havoc and destruction from the Ouse to the Tees. Victorious, he constructed two wooden castles in the city on top of earth mounds, one on either side of the Ouse. Stone walls and gates were added in the thirteenth century, then a great Abbey and Priory, several friaries and nunneries were founded, and over forty churches, as York became one of the main religious centres of England.

The church exercised tremendous power over people's lives, as the city prospered as a port and became a 'staple town' for wool, England's chief export. Samples were brought to the newly built 'Merchant Adventurers Hall' to be weighed, and every trade then had its 'guild', and the city was covered by 'guild halls' where members met and traded.

York became the northern capital of the whole of England, visited by many Kings and Queens. Indeed 'The Duke of York' became the title of the sovereign's second son, a tradition which has endured until modern times. Despite the turbulence of this period in history, and later often misguided restoration, many of the medieval treasures have survived to allow visitors to become acquainted with the life and art of the era.

*Drunken Monk*

In the gardens of the Yorkshire Museum lie the thirteenth-century ruins of St Mary's Abbey. At one time the Abbey rivalled the Minster in importance, and to this day its tranquil setting in the centre of the bustling city gives a clue as to what must have attracted the Benedictine monks here back in 1088. Despite its peaceful setting, some of the monks considered the discipline too lax, and soon left to form a much stricter monastery.

The pardoning of Brother Jocundius may well have contributed to their exodus. According to the story, in the Middle Ages there was a young novice monk at St Leonard's Hospital called Jocundius. One day he went out into the town, visited the fair, and succumbed to the temptations of the demon drink. He was found drunk by two of his brethren, and taken back to St Leonard's. For this grave breach of his monastic vows he was sentenced to be bricked up alive in his cell. His fellow monks carried out the sentence, and left Jocundius sealed in his cell, to face a long lingering death. Devastated, he slumped down against the wall, and being a heavy man it gave way under his weight. He fell through the wall and into the grounds of the adjoining St Mary's Abbey.

*Old Habits Die Hard*

Still dressed in his novice's robes, Jocundius was mistaken as a novice from St Mary's Abbey, and soon accepted by the brethren. Time passed and as the years progressed, his jovial nature endeared him to all, and he was eventually promoted to the post of cellarer, in charge of the beer and wine cellars of the Abbey. One day he went to test the wine for a feast and failed to return, and unfortunately he once again succumbed to his old temptation and was found in the cellar in an excessively drunken state. The punishment was again severe and he was bricked up alive a second time. He fell down drunk and again the wall gave way and this time he fell back into St Leonard's Hospital. In his inebriated state he began to sing cheerfully and was heard by some of the brethren. Now at first on seeing him they thought he was a ghost, but then realising that he was alive they hailed it as a miracle – Jocundius had risen from the dead! By a strange twist of fate, that very day the Prior of St Leonard's had died, and Jocundius' return from the dead could only mean one thing – he was destined by God to be their new Prior. So he was duly elected, and ruled for many years with a firm but kindly hand.

*Impregnable Walls*

York's impressive walls, built on earthen ramparts around the city, were begun around 1250. The ever present threat of attack from Scottish raiding parties, in particular the armies of William Wallace and Robert the Bruce, prompted a major building programme in the thirteenth and fourteenth centuries, which also included the strengthening of the city gates. During these campaigns against the Scottish rebels both Edward I and his son Edward II made York their war capital, and once the royal household and its treasury had taken up residence impregnability took on great importance. Today York's famous walls offer an amazing elevated walkway and vantage point for some of the best panoramic views of the modern city.

Above left: *York's impressive walls, built on earthen ramparts around the city, were begun around 1250.*

Above right: *The Mansion House, home to the Lord Mayors of York.*

*Tudor and Stuart York*

York was destined to play an important part in the War of the Roses. In 1486 Elizabeth of York married Henry VII. Their union brought the two warring houses of York and Lancaster together and is commemorated in the famous Rose Window in York Minster. In the sixteenth century the King's Council governed the North of England from York from its seat at King's Manor, which at that time was within the grounds of the old St Mary's Abbey. York continued to be an important city for trade and commerce until the seventeenth century when the Civil War disrupted this growth of prosperity. Instead York became a city subjected to attack and then capture in 1644 by Oliver Cromwell's Parliamentarians. The Jacobite Rebellion of 1745 was the last occasion that traitors' heads were exhibited on Micklegate Bar, one of the four principal gateways to the city of York.

*Georgian York – the Social Capital of the North*

By Georgian times the city had become an important coaching centre (with daily transport links to both north and south), still flourishing as a market town but with less concentration on the use of the river Ouse as a means of transporting goods. To accommodate the increasing road traffic, the city's streets were widened, giving improved access to places such as the newly erected Grand Assembly Rooms built by Lord Burlington in 1732, and Mansion House, home to the Lord Mayor of York. The growing city once again became an elegant centre of fashion and also a centre of craftsmanship. The racecourse was built, and horse-racing was established; the Assembly Rooms were built, and wealthy people from all over northern England built fashionable town houses in the newly widened streets, particularly in the Bootham, Blossom Street and Micklegate areas of the city.

*Victorian York*

Prosperity and squalor rubbed shoulders with each other as the city's population expanded. The dreaded cholera broke out in 1832 and again in 1848. Typhoid Fever struck in 1847, probably caused by insanitary conditions throughout the city at that time. York's population expanded from an estimated 12,000 in the eighteenth century to nearly 70,000 by the end of the nineteenth century. This massive increase in population inevitably brought dramatic changes to the city. The much-needed changes included new roads, bridges and buildings in order to accommodate the increasing traffic and need for housing.

*There's a Train Coming!*

The nineteenth century saw York largely untouched by the Industrial Revolution which was so dramatically changing other parts of the country, until an enterprising draper by the name of George Hudson, a Lord Mayor of the city, and a Member of Parliament, became one of the early investors in the railway building boom during the 1830s and '40s. His shrewd investments were to make him into a millionaire, and he became known as 'The Railway King'. Within just ten short years he had fallen from power when irregularities in his dealings were discovered, and he died in relative poverty in 1871. His foresight made York a leading railway centre, and in many ways laid the foundations for its present prosperity. In 1877 a station was built for the new form of transport, the steam engine. The railway had arrived in York. Sadly, the only significant remaining Victorian buildings still standing in York are the Royal York Hotel and York station, which was designed by Thomas Prosser. Today, as a reminder of the past, York's National Railway Museum celebrates railways from the 1820s to the present day.

Above left: *As you wander the narrow streets, riverside walks and peaceful gardens you are never far away from those who have gone before.*

Above right: *A ghostly figure with a score to settle is in residence in just about every deserted street or dark ginnel in the old town.*

*Modern York*

The most amazing thing about the city is its never-ending ability to reinvent itself. Now a vibrant and leading tourist attraction famous throughout the world, as you wander the narrow streets, riverside walks and peaceful gardens you are never far away from those who have gone before, each of whom has played their part in the city's distinct history. Music and theatre fill much of York's festival calendar; buskers and young actors entertain the tourists on street corners, as they enjoy shopping in the traffic-free streets and shops within the confines of the city's medieval walls.

*The Darker Side of York*

However, the city also has a darker side: with its long history of conflict and many tragic events, it boasts more than its fair share of ghosts, ghouls, phantoms and things that go bump in the night. In fact, York claims to be 'Europe's most haunted city' and sometimes it seems as though a ghostly figure with a score to settle is in residence in just about every deserted street or dark ginnel in the old town. As darkness falls a multitude of award-winning guides are available to take the bolder visitors on a chilling journey to discover some of York's more spine-tingling secrets. Join me if you will, as through this book we discover some of the ghosts and gravestones of York...

# Chapter 2
# Haunted Places

## *The Minster*

York Minster, begun in 1220, is world renowned, and is without doubt the finest amongst the city's many religious remains. Its varying architectural details span a period of 252 years of construction; they include a number of ornate tombs and intricate stained glass windows. Whilst the Minster may be the jewel in the crown amongst York's many buildings, a visit to some of the forty fine Norman churches may prove equally rewarding. Many interesting antiquities are to be found, from fonts to lecterns to monuments. Prime amongst these are undoubtedly the stained and painted glass windows, of which almost every church has superb examples.

*Built Askew!*
The South Transept is oldest part of the Minster which is above ground. Under the Minster is the Roman headquarters building, which is at roughly 45 degrees to the present building. This Roman building, which is believed to have been the basis of Edwin's wooden church and palace in AD 627, and is on the alignment of Petergate and St Michael-le-Belfry church, has given the Minster problems over the centuries. The Norman cathedral built by Archbishop Thomas of Bayeux in 1080 was askew across the hard Roman foundations and has been unstable round the Tower Crossing ever since. The original stone Anglo-Saxon cathedral destroyed by the Normans was probably north of the Minster in Dean's Park.

*And Off-Centre!*
In the thirteenth century, Archbishop Walter de Grey started the rebuilding of the South Transept, which started a process by which the Norman cathedral was progressively rebuilt over the next 252 years. The South Transept was built almost a metre off-centre due to the presence of earlier buildings; this is clearly visible in the windows of the South Wall which include the famous Rose Window. The Transept also does not meet the Tower Arch centrally but is also around a metre off-centre. It is believed that the North Transept was built to the designs of just one Master Mason, who designed it from top to bottom with the superb Five Sisters Window as a centrepiece inside and out. The North Transept is also off-centre like the south but this is concealed far more skilfully.

*Toilet up the Tower*
The present Chapter House was built slightly askew to the rest of the Minster – this is most obvious in the doorway into the Chapter House which is at a slightly different angle to the Vestibule. In the Middle Ages, the Minster was painted with bright colours inside – traces of red, blue and gold paint and heraldic designs are clearly visible in the Chapter House Vestibule.

The top storey of the Vestibule was used as a mason's drawing office – they probably realised there was a good bit of work in York so they might as well make themselves comfortable! The

*The Minster's varying architectural details span a period of 252 years of construction.*

drawing office was provided with a fireplace and garderobe flushed by water from a gargoyle! Today modern Minster employees complain that there is no toilet up the Tower, where they have to sit on duty for hours on end, yet the thirteenth-century masons suffered no such inconvenience.

*Wicked Caricatures*

The Chapter House is a remarkable piece of engineering as the walls are almost all window – the weight of the vault is taken upwards by great vertical timbers in the roof; the weight is then transferred sideways by huge beams and then downwards clear of the walls by flying buttresses. The huge roof and vault were prefabricated, as the timbers in the roof still have the markings on, indicating which timber was to join which. The great roof trusses were most probably fabricated on the ground, marked up, dismantled, hoisted up and then re-assembled. The Chapter House carvings – all once painted – are very amusing, and are mainly original; Victorian replacements stand out clearly. Some are undoubtedly caricatures and some are very wicked. Scenes include a man sticking his tongue out, a loving couple cuddling, an eagle pecking a man's eyes out, a cat chasing a mouse (in the style of modern cartoon characters, Tom and Jerry), a talkative woman with her mouth tied up, a man having his tongue bitten by lizards, a peeping tom with his eyes blindfolded, and a man doing something very strange to a sheep. What these represent is not certain, but in the Middle Ages the high ceilings were painted with scenes of heaven and the saints, as were the stained glass windows; perhaps these carvings represent the sin and wickedness of earth while above was sinless heaven.

*The Weakest Go to the Wall*

The Nave was designed initially by Simon le Mason – the first Master Mason whose name we know. He seems to have conceived the idea of building a completely new Nave to replace the original Norman one; in the event his designs were changed as the building rose due to the inordinate time it took to finish the Nave – almost seventy years. During the building, work was held up by the Black Death, war with Scotland and shortage of money. One of the problems of building in the Middle Ages was getting a level building. It was relatively easy to build a straight wall using a plumb bob and a level wall using a level with a dangling string. But how did you ensure the two outside walls were rising from the same starting height and at the same level? The answer is a trough of water, which acted a giant spirit level. But in the new Nave of York,

*The carvings are undoubtedly caricatures and some are very wicked.*

Simon le Mason could not use the trough as the old Norman Nave was in the way. So the two outside walls rose up with about thirty centimetres difference in their height, with the north wall lower than the south. This is visible in the wall benches, put for the old to sit on, hence 'the weakest go to the wall'. In the eighteenth century the Nave was re-floored level, whereas before it had sloped downwards south to north. This covered the bottom foot or so of the wall benches and also the bases of the aisle columns, which had therefore to be provided with false bases.

*William de Hoton's 'Bad Peg Day'*

By the mid-fourteenth century, the early Gothic Choir built in 1160, was perceived as old-fashioned, and it was decided in 1361 that it should be rebuilt. When he started laying out the new Choir from the east, the old Norman Choir was still standing and in the way of a sight line to the Tower. So, when William de Hoton put his pegs in the ground in 1361, he got them in slightly askew, so that over the next sixty years, as the Choir advanced westwards, finally being completed about 1420, it got more and more out of true, to the north. By the time in the early fifteenth century when the new Choir met the Tower Arch, it was about a metre too far north, hence the misalignment visible from the Nave. This is also very visible on the west wall of the Choir where it meets the Tower Arch, with more columns on the left than the right. To compound the problems, the east end foundation was laid on sand, and much of the rest of the Choir on hard Roman buildings, so it gradually began to lean out. The masons just carried on building with the result that the top is overhanging by over a metre. Fortunately it is tied back into the building; it was all underpinned 1967-72. Also the eastern bay of the Lady Chapel is wedge-shaped, being wider at the east than the west!

*Tumbling Tower!*

Work also seems to have started on heightening the Central Tower early in the fifteenth century. We believe that there were thirty-seven Master Masons and seven carpenters, plus labourers, working at the Minster in 1419. They were divided in two teams: one working on finishing the Choir and the other on the Central Tower. It was during the rebuilding of the Central Tower that disaster struck in 1407. From about 1400, work seems to have been going on to rebuild the Central Bell Tower, which had a wooden lead-sheathed spire. Its collapse came in 1407, in on itself, rather than toppling sideways, causing the pillars round the crossing to lean; this is clearly visible in all the pillars near the Tower, while the North Transept West Clerestory is buckled and bent from the collapse. The collapse was blamed on the carelessness of the masons. What had happened is that over the previous century the old Norman tower, which had been buttressed at each corner pillar by solid walls, had these walls removed to make openings to the new Nave and choir aisles. The collapse was inevitable.

*Consecrated but Not Completed*

In about 1460 it was decided to add a Lantern Stage to the incomplete Central Tower. It may have been intended to make it higher still, but in 1472 the Minster authorities decided that work had gone on for long enough, and so the Central Tower was left incomplete – hence its cut-off straight appearance – and the Minster was consecrated on St Peter's Day, 3 July 1472. However the Master Mason, William Hyndeley, was still busily carving crockets and pinnacles right up until the mid-1480s!

*Men with their legs crossed in agony for the loo. In the Middle Ages, these carved figures would have piddled all over you when it rained, as they had water spouts!*

*Rude Gargoyles*

The stone yard is visible through its main doors. In the Middle Ages the stone, magnesian limestone from Stutton near Tadcaster, was brought in great blocks by water, and dragged up Stonegate – hence its name. In more recent years the Tadcaster quarries were exhausted and the stone came from Cadeby near Doncaster from the same geological bed of limestone as was originally used. Recently, the quarries at Stutton near the original one have been reopened on a small scale and are once again able to provide the stone. The stone is now cut into blocks on the big circular stone saw, profiled on another saw, taken through the red doors to be carved with power tools. Finally it is carved into gargoyles etc. in the carver's shop overlooking Deangate. There are some very fine rude gargoyles on the south-east corner of the Choir. They depict men with their legs crossed in agony for the loo, which in the Middle Ages would have piddled all over you when it rained, as they had water spouts! There is a joke in York that if the Minster is ever seen free from scaffolding, the Roman Catholic Church will have it back, but they never will, as there are about forty people employed in the stone yard and there is an indefinite ongoing programme of restoration and repair.

*Stone Carver's Revenge*

The carvings around the Great West Door were designed by Rory Young of Cirencester and executed by the Minster masons in 1988. The carvings depict the Genesis Cycle from Adam and Eve on the left to the sacrifice of Isaac by Abraham on the right. Also on the right of the carving of Abraham and the three angels is a carving of a man tipping slops out of a chamber pot on a Scottish bagpiper! The man who carved this used to live opposite and hated the droning of the bagpipes of a Scottish busker who used to play outside his window. So he has got his own back by showing him being perpetually showered in sewage!

*The Ghosts Within*

An account published in the middle of last century tells of a strange haunting experienced by a group of people who were viewing the Minster one warm summer's evening when it was busy with visitors. Two of the group, a lady and a gentleman, had become separated from the rest of their friends. As they stood admiring the architecture they noticed a man standing near to them in full naval uniform, who appeared to be staring intently at the lady, as the gentleman looked from the man in uniform to his companion he was astonished to see an immediate paleness, and signs of considerable agitation in her face, which increased as the figure became more distinct in the evening gloom of the cathedral. The figure approached, and walked slowly and deliberately across to the pair. When it reached the lady the figure leaned over to her and whispered in a low and barely audible voice, 'there is a future state', turned, and moved swiftly away into the aisle of the Minster. Astonished at the encounter, which to him had no obvious explanation, her companion attempted to catch up with the retreating figure, to ask for an explanation, but it had simply disappeared into the crowds of evening strollers outside.

*Childhood Pact*

Back inside the Minster he found that his lady companion had managed to relocate the group of friends from whom they had been separated earlier in the evening. She seemed to have regained her composure and looked far less pale and agitated then when he had left her a few moments ago. She was trying to explain to them what had happened just a few moments earlier. Like many people she was interested in the possibility of life after death and related that as a child she had made a pact with her brother, with whom she was very close, to the effect that whoever died first would appear to the other, to show that the afterlife was more than a fantasy. Many years had passed; her brother had joined the Royal Navy, and she had forgotten all about the agreement until just a few moments ago, when she had clearly seen him in full uniform in the Minster. Despite assurances from her friends that she must have been mistaken, she insisted that the man had been her brother, and she recounted the words which he had spoken. She added, 'the instant he uttered those words my fears were confirmed; I knew my poor brother was dead and what I looked at was only his ghost or shadow'.

The family was officially informed a few weeks later of the man's death, and the time and date given in the communiqué were determined to be exactly the same as his sister's experience in the Minster on that fateful summer's evening.

*The Haunted Pew*

Another haunting story attached to the Minster relates to a man by the name of Dean Gale, who cared for the cathedral in the latter years of the seventeenth century. He was well loved and known for his devotion to the Minster and worked tirelessly to preserve and enhance its ancient grandeur. Never did he neglect his religious duties, and contentiously attended as many services as possible, always occupying the same pew. In the year 1702, Dean Gale died, and his passing was greatly mourned, a deep sadness felt by everyone connected with the Minster. He was laid to rest in a fine tomb, which can be seen to this day. Not long after his death, a local preacher climbed into the pulpit to deliver a sermon as part of a regular service. The worshippers who attended were surprised when the usually eloquent minister stood dumbstruck for what must have seemed like an eternity before the hushed congregation, before hesitantly beginning his sermon. On climbing down from the pulpit the pale-faced minister shakily announced that Dean Gale was in his pew and listening to his service. Ever since that day there have been reports of the sighting of the phantom of Dean Gale sitting listening attentively to the services in the Minster.

*The pale-faced minister shakily announced that Dean Gale was in his pew and listening to his service.*

*Ancient Policemen*

The office of Minster Policeman derives from that of the Constable of the Liberty – a post which goes back into antiquity and was similar to that of Parish Constable. In 1285 the Minster Close was enclosed by a stone wall some four meters high: within this wall the Dean and Chapter were the law. Until 1839 they had a Liberty of their own, it was called the Liberty of Saint Peter and Peter Prison, with its own chief constable, constables, coroners, magistrates, bailiffs, stewards and under-stewards.

Minster constables had existed long before the great fire which devastated the building in 1829, started by the insane Jonathan Martin late one night. However, the fire represented a turning point in the care of the building. At a Chapter meeting on 6 March 1829, the Dean and Chapter decreed that 'henceforward a watchman/constable shall be employed to keep watch every night in and about the cathedral'. The new watchman could have been one Thomas Marshall, although the first record of his name appears when the Liberty of St Peter and Peter Prison was abolished in 1839 and its jurisdiction passed to the civil corporation. We know Marshall was employed by the Dean and Chapter until 1854, on a salary of forty-one pounds and twelve shillings per year.

The title of Minster Police first occurs in 1855 when William Gladin replaced Thomas Marshall. The fact that Gladin's name replaced Marshall's directly in the records suggests that the latter's post of Constable of the Liberty was identifiable with that of Gladin's post of Minster Policeman. If such a conclusion can indeed be drawn, it means that the post of Minster Police Officer precedes the establishment of Sir Robert Peel's modern day Police Constabulary. In fact, Sir Robert Peel is believed to have examined the Minster Police prior to forming the British police force. Hardly surprising, as his sister was married to the then Dean, William Cockburn, and on some of his family visits to York, he would surely have observed the Minster Police at work. Today, the modern Minster Police watch over upwards of 2,000 people at any one time, dealing efficiently and effectively with whatever problems may arise on a daily basis. At night they patrol the streets around the base of the Minster, taking care of Minster property and keeping order, sometimes a dangerous and challenging job, requiring patience and good humour. They operate from a new police office which has recently opened off the North Choir Aisle marked by two old-fashioned truncheons hanging next to the door.

*Old Gladin's Nightmare Encounter*

The story is told of William Gladin who had the reputation of being a most prosaic and unimaginative old man, and always took his dog along with him when he was working on night duty in the Minster. One cold winter's night in 1879, he was sitting on a bench in the Nave of the Minster, when his dog suddenly jumped up and bolted in the direction of the North Transept. Gladin got up to follow, truncheon in hand, fully expecting to discover some intruder hiding in the darkness of the building. As he crossed, his attention was caught by a curious apparition under the north-west tower; it was a shaft of blue light, about the same height as a man, which passed slowly to the centre of the Great West Door before gliding up the centre aisle. Unafraid, Gladin followed the apparition, and saw it crossing to the South Transept. Here in the east corner, the strange light remained for at least ten minutes before flickering away, apparently through the stones in the wall. Eventually, strangely puzzled, Gladin went in search of his dog: he discovered it cowering by the door, whimpering and shivering in sheer terror, and as soon as he opened the door it bolted past him. From that day forth it could never again be persuaded to enter the Minster. Whenever anyone suggested to the old policeman that his experience on that cold winter's night was just a dream, he would chuckle and reply, 'well tha mun ask t' dog. T' dog knaws!'

*The most stately and complete prison of any in the kingdom, if not in Europe.*

## York Castle Museum

*Long term Prison*

Prisoners have been housed in the castle since the thirteenth century, but by the early eighteenth century many parts of the buildings had fallen into poor repair, and it was decided that the time had come to build a new county gaol.

Stone was reused from many of the more ruinous parts of the old castle, and also from the nearby Kings Manor.

*Model Jail?*

By the year 1705 the new gaol was completed, having taken four years to build. The architect is unknown, but it was possibly William Wakefield, a trained lawyer rather than a professional architect. A native of Yorkshire, Wakefield also designed Duncombe Park and Gilling Castle.

It was designed to house felons – the men and women of Yorkshire who were accused of the most serious crimes. It would also accommodate debtors (those who were unfortunate enough to have fallen into debt and to be imprisoned on the instigation of their creditors). The building was set out to be both modern and functional. Men and women were to be housed separately, as were those awaiting trial and those already convicted.

The debtors were housed in the upper floors; the right-hand wing housed the chapel and the left-hand wing the governor of the gaol. At the very lowest level, flanked by earthly justice in the form of the governor and divine justice by the chapel, were housed the felons. Separate outside exercise yards were provided for each type of inmate.

At the time it was believed by some to be an excellent prison. Preacher John Wesley, who visited two inmates in 1759, later wrote that he found it 'a most commodious prison', and Daniel Defoe once described it as 'the most stately and complete prison of any in the kingdom, if not in Europe, kept as neat within side as it is noble without'.

*Manacles Charged Extra*

However, the harsh reality was that conditions in the gaol were far from ideal. The warders were unpaid, earning their living by selling to the inmates whatever meagre extras they could afford, and prisoners' clothing and possessions were often taken away and pawned. The cells were devoid of sunlight, and inmates slept two or more to an iron mesh bed with only a thin straw mattress, without sheets, in a cramped cell no more than a couple of meters square. Most of the time they remained locked in their cells for up to sixteen hours at a time. Some of the more dangerous prisoners were kept chained in irons, the weight of which could exceed thirteen kilos. During the sixteenth century, Catholic recusants were even charged for the use of their manacles according to their status – ten shillings for a yeoman, twenty shillings for a gentleman and forty shillings for an esquire.

In the overcrowded and unsanitary living conditions illness and disease were common. The most feared was typhus; sometimes called 'Jail Fever', it was a disease of the slums. It was also often found on board ships, and whenever people were forced to live together in very overcrowded and unsanitary conditions. Poor diet and overwork made the working classes more susceptible to it. As a result it was treated as a less urgent problem than cholera, which during the nineteenth century struck the rich as well as the poor.

*Debtors' Prison*

In the eighteenth century almost half of the prison population were debtors. Both men and women were imprisoned by their creditors. Whilst in prison their property was protected, and they were encouraged to work to help to clear their debts. As civil prisoners they were allowed far more privileges than the common felons housed in other parts of the gaol. During the hours of daylight they were allowed to entertain visitors, friends and family, and they were even allowed their own food, furniture and personal possessions. Of course, many could not afford to pay for even the basics, and so had rely on the allowance of food paid for by the county; some of the most destitute remained imprisoned for many years, and a number eventually died in prison.

Until changes in the law in 1815, debtors could be liable for the costs of their room and bedding, but the law stated that if they escaped then the gaoler could become liable for all their bills including their debts! During the nineteenth century the insolvency laws were revised, and in 1844 imprisonment for debts of under £20 was stopped. All debtors ceased to be imprisoned in 1869.

*The New Drop*

In 1801 public opinion was changing, and many seemingly religious and compassionate members of society were unhappy with the spectacle of public hangings which had taken place at Tyburn at the Knavesmire for the previous 422 years. It was decided that a new gallows should be erected at the rear of the gaol for the execution of its inmates, who would walk straight from the condemned cell to their appointment with the scaffold - a dramatic change from the earlier custom of parading them through the streets of the city in an open cart, with numerous stops to call at local inns on the way to have their souls strengthened and tongues loosened by benevolent landlords.

All of this was carried out with the hope that the condemned man or woman would entertain the bawdy crowd waiting at the Knavesmire with a salacious confession, and on a good day go on to regale their cheering audience with a rousing farewell speech, before their dance of death at the end of the hemp. The time for the old ways had come to an end, and with a certain lack of imagination the new gallows at the rear of the gaol were christened 'The New Drop'.

*Race Days Were Never the Same*

Executions were still open to the public, but the more sensitive of York's elegant ladies and gentlemen would no longer be forced to watch the common villains dancing at the end of the hemp on race days. However, many still attended public executions, and it became necessary to widen Castlegate Postern to a width of eight metres to allow for public viewing. The day of 9 August 1856 witnessed the largest ever gathering for an execution at The New Drop, when a crowd in excess of 15,000 gathered for the hanging of William Dove for the murder of his wife.

*Tyburn Gaol.*

Just twelve years later following an Act of Parliament, public executions at the site came to an end with the hanging of Frederick Parker, who following his release from Beverley Prison, killed his companion, Daniel Driscol, with a hedge stake. From that time forth the only visible indication to the citizens of York of an execution taking place was a black flag hoisted high above Clifford's Tower at the time of the execution.

*The Ghosts Within*

For many years local guide books and researchers have told of York Castle's grisly history. Visitors and staff members alike have claimed unusual experiences, of hearing the sound of screaming, and many dark figures have been seen wandering the cells and half-moon court.

On some occasions strange shadows are said to appear next to the site of The New Drop, near the exterior wall facing Castle Mills Bridge. A number of museum staff have reported a litany of mysterious phenomena over the years, including the slamming shut of cell doors, the rattling of chains, and ghostly whispering voices. In the cell area a museum guide once claimed to have heard the sound of scratching in the corner of a cell, only to find the word 'innocent' scratched deeply into the flagstone floor.

## *York Theatre Royal*

The history of the theatre company can be traced back to a group of players which was founded by Thomas Keregan and first performed in the Merchant Taylor's Hall from around 1715. Some nineteen years later the company moved to a courtyard on the south side of the Minster, and in a further ten years to its present site. Enjoying continuing success, the theatre was substantially rebuilt twenty years after the move under the direction of its adventurous and ambitious manager, Joseph Baker.

By 1769, Baker's successor Tate Wilkinson was granted the respectability of a Royal Patent by George III, at the considerable cost of £500, and the players of the city of York became York Theatre Royal.

*York Theatre Royal.*

*The Grey Lady*

The area around Petergate Bar is often troubled by the enigmatic phantom of a lady dressed in grey. Also seen at various locations throughout the city, many different accounts of her past are told in York.

Some say that she was a nun, bricked up in a cellar centuries ago by vengeful authorities for her crimes against religious orthodoxy. Other accounts relate that she fell in love with a townsman, and breaking her vows of chastity became pregnant: she was expelled from her order, and disgraced. Her lover deserted her, and she was shunned by her family. Alone and desperate, she took her own life. Some versions tell of the young nun receiving a vision of an angel. For some reason, the visitation angered her superiors so much that they ordered her immediate expulsion from their order, and she died of a broken heart.

*The Mystery Remains*

A further account tells of the nun working at St Leonard's Hospital, the crypt of which has served as a theatre clubroom and social centre. At some time during the long history of the hospital, a young nun, whose name and life remain unknown, is said to have been walled up alive. The traditional site of her ordeal is in the wall of a dressing room behind the dress circle. This room was originally accessed by a spiral staircase, and was very small and cramped, prior to recent alterations to the theatre.

A number of occupants of this room have mentioned the strange sensation of being watched whilst they prepared for performances, whilst others noted a strange coldness which seemed to linger on. Many of the actresses who were given this room often asked to change it for another without any rational explanation for the request.

However the nun came to her death, she remains one of the more active ghosts in York, most often appearing as a lady dressed in the long flowing costume of her religious order.

*Music Lover?*

She has most frequently been seen in the Theatre Royal, usually in the dress circle, though why a medieval nun should appear in a theatre, which was built in 1744, is a mystery. Perhaps she is hoping to find herself a good seat, just in case the theatre ever puts on a production of *The Sound of Music.*

## *The Shrine of Margaret Clitherow*

*The Shambles*

The oldest street in York, it had a mention in the Domesday Book. Traditionally it was the street of the butchers, and old records tell us that in 1872 there were twenty-six butchers trading from premises in this street. Over the years the street has had a number of name changes, originally in 1240 it was known as 'Haymongergate', than later as 'Nedlergate', followed by 'The Fleshammels' (the street of butchers) which was finally shortened to its present name in around 1500. Famous now for its array of smart shops, it presents a picture of 'olde worlde' charm with its narrow width and its overhanging upper storeys, and bustling crowds of international tourists.

*Bloody, Stinking Mess*

However had you visited this street, 300 years ago, it would have been a very different experience! Carcasses of animals would have been hung from the hooks above the windows, and large cuts of meat displayed on the shelves below. Livestock would have been kept behind the shops and slaughtered on site.

*The Shambles – in former times blood and waste were washed out by butchers from their shops and slaughterhouses.*

*The shrine of the Catholic martyr Margaret Clitherow.*

Later, when York opened its own cattle market it meant that cattle were no longer housed behind the shops. However, the slaughterhouses remained, and the cattle were driven in on foot from the market to the street's many slaughterhouses. Down the middle of street would have been an open gutter to carry away the blood and waste washed out by the butchers from the shops and slaughterhouses into the street.

Also, domestic waste from chamber pots would have been thrown down from the windows above to either drain into open ditches, or stagnate in the road. Manure was collected at night, but no great effort was made to take it very far away.

The foul unhygienic conditions led to several outbreaks of cholera and typhus, and yet it was not until the twentieth century that significant changes were eventually made.

*Dangerous Times*

The Shambles in York is the street where there lived a famous Catholic martyr named Margaret Clitherow; her shrine is in Nos 35-36. Margaret Middleton married John Clitherow, a widowed butcher who had his business at No. 35 The Shambles.

Following her marriage, Margaret became an enthusiastic convert to Catholicism. These were turbulent times in the religious world, with the Dissolution of the monasteries under Henry VIII and continued religious warring throughout the reigns of his children.

Margaret began to lead a brave and dangerous life, by hiding and sheltering travelling priests, and conducting Mass for local Catholics in her home. Warned and imprisoned for her continual refusal to conform to the Protestant way of life, she continued with her activities to the annoyance of the authorities. The inspectors would count the windows outside the houses and compare them to the count inside, to see if an area had been concealed in which to hide a priest.

*A Pressing Engagement*

In 1586, on the evidence of a frightened child, the authorities arrested Margaret and charged her with providing cover for the priests and with practising Catholicism. She was offered a trial, but she insisted she had no crime to answer to, and so was sentenced to the process known as *piene forte dure*, reserved exclusively for those who refused to plead to the charges laid before them. The accused was spread-eagled and pegged to the floor, with a sharp stone placed beneath their back. A heavy board or door was placed on top of them, and one by one heavy stones loaded on to it until, finally unable to bear the crushing weight, the poor soul eventually answered the charge. This cruel form of punishment and torture almost always resulted in the painful death of the victim.

*Death of a Martyr*
After being deprived of food for several days, and only allowed 'puddle water' for her thirst, Margaret was taken to the toll booth on the Ouse Bridge, where it is said she was crushed beneath 8 hundredweight of rock, causing her ribs to break through the skin. The whole process took fifteen minutes. In her final screams she called for the mercy of her lord.

Her house is now a shrine in The Shambles, and numerous visitors have remarked on the uncanny peace and stillness that surrounds her home; despite its front door opening onto one of the busiest streets in the whole of York. She was canonised on 25 October 1970, and her right hand can still be seen in the Bar Convent Museum in York.

## *Raffles Tea Room – Stonegate*

*The Doctor's Daughter*
According to old stories, the tall and narrow building which now houses Raffles Tea Rooms was many years ago both the home and workplace of a successful and celebrated Victorian doctor and his family. In a small room at the very top of the old house lived the doctor's youngest daughter, 'the apple of his eye'. She was around six years of age, and her friendly character and stunning long blond hair made her a favourite with both the servants and the many patients who called at the house.

As the doctor's practice flourished he often entertained many of his influential friends and patients with lavish dinner parties at the house. At one such gathering, his young daughter was duly introduced to the assembled guests before being sent off with one of the servants to her attic bedroom. Understandably, she resented being packed off to bed in the midst of the excitement, but obediently trudged up the three flights of stairs which led to her bedroom. The servant duly tucked her up in bed and returned downstairs to her duties, looking after the doctor and his merry guests.

Throughout the evening his daughter lay awake in bed, listening to the sounds of merriment from the dinner party in the house below, wishing that she could return. Eventually, she could contain herself no longer and crept out onto the attic landing to listen to the tinkle of glasses and the happy murmur of conversation which floated up the staircase from the guests below.

*Horror on the Stairs*
As she leaned forward in an attempt to hear more of what was being said, her tiny hand slipped from the polished bannister, and she tumbled head over heels to her death in the dark cellar, four storeys below. Many years later her tiny footsteps can still be heard on the slow climb to her former bedroom. Her phantom has been reported, sitting on a shop counter – 'a pretty little Victorian girl, with the most incredibly blond hair you have ever seen'.

## *Bedern – Nightmare in the Orphanage*

*The Choir Move Out*
Bedern, off Goodramgate, was the medieval home of the Minster's vicars choral from around 1574. The building was also used for the care of elderly and infirm people, who were granted by the city a small pension. The old people eventually moved out in 1847 and the whole

*Bedern, where the York Industrial Ragged School was located.*

area degenerated into an area of slums, warehouses and small workshops. The slums were mostly occupied by the poor Irish immigrants – the majority of whom had only one room for themselves and their large families.

*The Poor Orphans Move In*

By the mid-nineteenth century, a chilling type of orphanage-cum-workhouse was established on the site. It was known as the 'York Industrial Ragged School'. Its master, who had the reputation of a man of cruel temperament and ferocious nature, was paid well to round up local waifs and strays and put them hard to work. The avaricious man paid out as little as possible on food and clothing for his downtrodden workforce. His miserable charges died in great numbers from starvation, disease, exposure and neglect.

Although the orphans of the ragged school rarely survived for long, this was of little concern to the master; his unpaid workers were easily replaced by more waifs and strays, rounded up from the endless supply of homeless orphans wandering daily through York's shabby slums and alleyways.

*Secret of the Locked Cupboard*

The master was often too lazy to dispose of the bodies of his unfortunate charges, preferring instead to lock them in a large cupboard at the rear of the workhouse, where they lay cold and stiff awaiting their graves until eventually the stench of the rotting bodies would force him to take action. Often in the harsh Yorkshire winters, which were so typical of the time, when the ground grew hard as a tombstone covered in snow, he was prevented from digging even the shallowest of graves, and the corpses would be left to rot, as everyday the stench of the putrefying flesh of the former workers filled the workhouse.

*The Nightmares Begin*

During his last winter at the workhouse, as the months passed and the bodies once again piled up in the locked cupboard, the master began to be troubled by his deeds. He became convinced that late at night he could hear the laughter of his long-dead charges as they played in the streets outside his workhouse – free at last. He would rise sleepily from his bed, and with flickering oil lamp in hand, go downstairs into the cold empty workhouse. Once downstairs his curiosity turned to fear, as he believed that he could hear the terrified screams of his unfortunate charges emanating from the stinking locked cupboard. Night after night he would hear the same sounds and it began to play on his guilty conscience.

*The Dreadful Night*

Late one night, as his weary charges slept in their cold, flea-ridden dormitory, he totally lost his reason and went completely mad. He ran through the building, a man possessed, massacring all the remaining half-sleeping children with a huge knife from the workhouse kitchen.

The authorities discovered him the next morning, whimpering amongst the heaps of mutilated bodies of his unfortunate charges. He was dragged off to the local asylum where he spent the rest of his days locked in solitary confinement. It is said that the only sound ever to come from his cell was that of him pleading over and over again with his young victims for forgiveness.

*Further Discoveries*

Eventually the workhouse was moved to a new location at the bottom of Marygate in 1855, and at the time it was reported that several more orphans' bodies were discovered in the house. Nervous locals for many years afterwards refused to enter the area of Bedern after dark. The restless spirits of the dead children are still occasionally seen playing in the midnight streets around the Bedern area.

*Late-Night Walk*

A number of years ago a local man who was in the habit of taking his dog on a late-night walk along Goodramgate reported that one moonlight night, as he was passing by the entrance to Bedern, he heard the sound of children's voices. Curious as to why children should be out so late, as the time was close to midnight, he turned under the archway. To his surprise his faithful dog growled and bristled, and refused to move forward no matter how hard he was encouraged, so his owner continued alone. Coming out at the other side of the archway, he was amazed as the sound of the playing children suddenly stopped, and search as he might he could find no trace of human activity.

Some months later the same man joined one of the conducted ghost tours of the city. At the end of the evening he thanked his guide for his stories, and in particular the accounts relating to Bedern for it seemed to throw some light on his own strange earlier experiences. Particularly interesting is the fact that prior to joining the group he knew nothing of the tradition of haunted Bedern.

## *St William's College*

This is one of York's most atmospheric buildings. Behind the imposing York Minster runs College Street, which during the eighteenth century was known as 'Little Alice Lane' (from a diminutive woman who once lived here) and before that as 'Vicar Lane'. Today College Street takes its name from St William's College, which stands about halfway up the street.

*Herbert's Bastard*

St William's College is dedicated to William Fitzherbert, the nephew of King Stephen and great-grandson of William the Conqueror. St William was born around 1100, the illegitimate son of William Fitzherbert, the King's Treasurer. His mother was Emma, the illegitimate daughter of the Count of Anjou and King Stephen's half-sister. So William was surnamed 'Fitzherbert', i.e. Herbert's bastard! He became a churchman and Treasurer of York Minster, residing in the Treasurer's House. He was a prime candidate for the position of Archbishop in 1142, helped no doubt by the fact that his uncle, Stephen, was King! Always a popular and hospitable man, well known for drinking, giving feasts and parties, he created enemies among the more ascetic wing of the Church, especially the Cistercians; they did not wish to have a free and easy, illegitimate royal nominee as Archbishop and wanted their own man for the job.

*Poison Pen Letter?*
A group of dissenters including the Abbots of Rievaulx and Fountains, the Priors of Guisborough and Kirkham, and the master of St Leonard's Hospital in York, all set out to Rome to make their objections known to Pope Innocent II. On route they called at Clairvaux to enlist the support of its Abbot, and although he did not join them on their journey to Rome he was happy to write a letter to the Pope which very clearly set out his views of William Fitzherbert. It read:

> Since many are called and few are chosen it is no great argument in favour of something doubtful that many may approve of it. The Archbishop of York is coming to see you – the same of whom I have repeatedly written to your Holiness. He is a man who puts not his trust in God his helper but hopes in abundance of his riches. His case is a weak and feeble one and I have it on the authority of truthful men that he is rotten from the soles of his feet to the crown of his head. What can this unrighteous man want with the arbiter of righteousness, the guardian of justice? Does he think he can swallow up righteousness in the Curia even as he had done in England the flooded river he drinks unconcerned; Jordan itself would have no terrors for his gaping mouth.

The following Lent of 1143, William Fitzherbert journeyed to Rome to let Pope Innocent II hear both sides of the argument, and he must have been successful, for he was consecrated Archbishop of York on 26 September of the same year.

*Sacked For Debauchery*
In 1145 when a new Pope, Eugenius III, was in power, the Cistercians, led by the Abbot of Fountains and St Bernard of Clairvaux, persuaded him to depose William in 1147, for alleged riotous living, debauchery and sexual incontinence. He was forced into exile with his uncle, the Bishop of Winchester, but appealed against his sacking.

*Friends in High Places?*
In 1153 the Pope, the Archbishop of York, the Abbot of Fountains and St Bernard of Clairvaux all died within the same year, struck down, some said, by the hand of God for their ill treatment of William. He was soon reinstated by the new Pope Anastasis IV and returned to York in triumph the following year. The entire city crowded onto Ouse Bridge to greet him on his return, thinking no doubt that party time had returned to York: the crowd was so great that the bridge collapsed, throwing them down into the cold river Ouse. William, who had already crossed the bridge, dropped to his knees and prayed on the far bank and they were all washed ashore by a miraculous tidal wave! The crowd was saved and people said he was a miracle worker.

*The Poisoned Chalice*
Less than a year later he was celebrating Mass at the High Altar of the Norman Minster, when he was taken ill and collapsed. He was taken to the nearby Archbishop's Palace where he died. It was soon claimed he had been murdered by a poisoned chalice, in a plot by the Cistercians. He was declared a saint and martyr, murdered at the altar of his own cathedral. This was a godsend to the Minster, which had six sainted Bishops and Archbishops, but not one of their bodies remained in York.

*Helped the Minster Get Ahead*
The body of a saint was considered essential to bring pilgrims and money. He was buried at the east end of the Nave, and before many months had passed, miracles occurred, attributed to

*The body of a saint was too good to keep in one place so the head of William Fitzherbert was removed and housed in a separate shrine in the Nave!*

his intervention – he was claimed to be particularly good at healing broken legs and curing blindness. In 1223 a strange, sweet-smelling oil was claimed to flow freely from his tomb. William was canonised in 1227 and a great shrine erected first in the Nave, then later in the new Choir of the Minster. The body of a saint was too good to keep in one place so his head was removed and housed in a separate shrine in the Nave! His shrine was later demolished by Henry VIII, but his body is now housed in a chapel in the crypt. Certainly one of the more colourful saints, perhaps the patron saint of boozers and party-goers! The main college was built between 1465 and 1467, and served as the home of the cathedral chantry priests. Not to be confused with singing vicars, chanting priests reserved their main vocal efforts until after sunset. Without doubt one of York's most atmospheric buildings, St William's College has a wealth of interesting features. Carved oak figures symbolising the labours of the months decorate the roof of the inner courtyard. An ancient sundial is on the right as you walk forward towards the semi-timbered building, which spans the street. This is all that remains of a covered way which Richard II allowed the vicars-choral to build so they could cross to Minster Yard without being molested. The building has also been used as a printing house and at one time housed the royal mint.

*Troublesome Priests*

The chantry priests of the Minster led a very relaxed lifestyle, having little to do apart from say Mass once or twice a day, and being comfortably paid young men they came to attract in York the reputation for often being more trouble than they were worth. It should be pointed out that these priests were usually not the appointed vicars-choral of the Minster, but were privately

*St William's College.*

employed and so were to a large extent outside the jurisdiction of the Minster authorities. There was little affection lost between the men of the Minster Liberty and the town, and consequently violent clashes commonly occurred, and there were a number of instances of murder. It was decided that these troublesome young priests needed somewhere to live where they would attract less attention, and St William's College was founded, established under the terms of a licence granted by Henry VI in 1455.

*Cutthroats in the Alleyway*

During the reign of Charles I, the college housed several wealthy clerics as well as a number of more humble lodgers, amongst them two brothers. Life could be hard in sixteenth-century York, and many a young lad down on his luck found a life of crime could sometimes be an easy way out of the gutter. Pickpockets (or 'fingersmiths') and cutthroats were commonplace amongst the dark and lonely alleys and snickleways of the city.

One dark moonless night the brothers, desperate to boost their meagre earnings, lurked with malicious intent in the shadows close to their lodgings in St William's College. The elder brother planned to rob one of the wealthy clergymen who frequented the area and persuaded his younger brother to help him in his dark deed. When a likely victim came into sight they pounced. He was to be a wealthy priest from the nearby Minster. The two sprang upon him, the elder brother slit his throat in the scuffle, and they made off with his purse and all the valuables they could find about his person.

*Brotherly Betrayal*

The younger brother was horrified by the turn of events and clutching the stolen purse fled back to their lodgings – he had been a reluctant partner from the start, and broke down in complete terror at the thought of both earthly and divine retribution. He locked himself and the priest's possessions inside an old ornate oak cabinet in St William's College.

The elder brother, fearing that his terrified sibling would break down and confess their crime, decided to tell all, and report him to the authorities, and betrayed his brother in return for a pardon. The younger and relatively blameless brother was immediately arrested, tried and hanged for murder. He never knew of his brother's betrayal and went to the gallows with no mention of his brother's involvement.

*An Eternity of Guilt*

The elder brother walked free from the law. He may have escaped the hangman's noose, but he could not escape his own conscience. He lived every day with the nagging and persistent demon of guilt over the betrayal of his brother. Sleep eluded him and night after night, week after week, his footsteps pounded the wooden floors of St William's College as he paced out his guilt. Then one night the footsteps were heard no more. The following morning the man was found dead in his room. His early death however failed to erase his guilt, for it is claimed that his footsteps can still be heard, late at night, as his unquiet spirit paces out for eternity.

## *Kings Manor – Exhibition Square*

*Many Uses*

This old building originated in AD 1208, as the property of St Mary's Abbey. During the Dissolution of the monasteries it passed to the Crown thus acquiring its present name. One of York's most historic buildings it has over the centuries served as a former Abbot's house, a royal dwelling, a fashionable seminary for genteel young ladies, and at one time assembly rooms. Many phantoms are claimed to wander the old building, including the black-cowled figure of a peaceful monk.

*Dying Roundheads*

Along the stone-flagged passage which leads from the inner courtyard to the old bowling green are claimed to linger the groans and screams of the dying Roundhead soldiers who were brought here following the unsuccessful attack on the manor on Trinity Sunday in 1644.

*Tudor Lady*

Also reported are sightings of a lady in a green Tudor costume who drifts peacefully through the ancient building; she appears to be carrying a bunch of blood-red roses. She is most often seen in the newest wing of the building, added as a Principal's House in 1900 by York architect Walter Brierley. There are accounts of a cleaner working in this part of the building one afternoon who was heard to scream loudly and was

*Many phantoms are claimed to wander the old building – including the black-cowled figure of a peaceful monk.*

*Kings Manor, where the Tudor Lady has been seen.*

discovered by staff in a fainting condition.She was later to tell of the reason for her distress – she had seen a lady come out from a cupboard and felt the figure walk straight through her. The phantom was described by the terrified girl as wearing a green dress of Tudor design, and carrying a bunch of blood-red ribbons. Over the following weeks the girl saw the figure again on a number of occasions, on each occasion at around the same time in the afternoon. As time went by she realised that the bunch of ribbons carried by the phantom was in fact a bunch of roses.

On one occasion the wife of a member of staff decided to keep watch with the girl and at the usual time during the afternoon the girl cried out, 'There she is. Can't you see her?' The disappointed staff member's wife saw nothing, but she did report hearing 'a swishing sound as of a very full-skirted dress, passing close by her'.

*The End of the Story?*

Eventually the cleaner left and returned home to her native Ireland; the Tudor lady was not seen again and interest waned. Sceptics often commented that the story could hardly be credible when the phantom had only ever been seen in the newest part of the building. How could it be that a lady wearing Tudor costume was only ever seen in a part of the building which never existed during Tudor times, and why on earth was she always seen carrying roses?

*Interesting Discovery*

That should be the end of the tale, but some time later John V. Mitchell, in his wonderful book *Ghosts of an Ancient City*, tells of an interesting discovery he made whilst browsing in a local bookshop: 'I discovered in a local bookshop a history of the building. This contained a manuscript plan, which had been made before the building of the new wing, and there, at right angles to the north-west side of the forecourt, appeared a long rectangle labelled "Former Rose Garden".'

Some locals claim that this may be the ghost of Anne Boleyn, who stayed here during her brief and tragic marriage to Henry VIII. Just why this identification was made is uncertain, and considering the large number of places this unhappy lady is believed to haunt; it might be more likely that the Lady in Green is in fact the phantom of some other less well known Tudor lady.

*'Off with his head, and set it on York gates, so York may overlook the town of York.'*

*The Final Twist to the Tale*

However, if indeed the phantom lady with the roses is Anne Boleyn there is one more twist to the tale. It is recorded that in 1523, as a teenager, she had fallen madly in love with Lord Henry Percy, later the 6th Earl of Northumberland and they had a semi-secret romance. Lord Henry's father, who had his eye on a rich heiress as his future daughter-in-law, ended the romance, and the heartbroken lovers were forced to go their separate ways.

Many years later when King Henry VIII was casting about for reasons to get rid of Anne Boleyn, her former lover Lord Henry Percy, despite pressure from his King, refused to discredit the lady by admitting that he had ever been involved with her, or that anything improper had ever taken place between them.

At her trial in 1536, Lord Henry Percy was said to be conspicuous by his absence, and her trial ended with her death sentence. She was beheaded at Tower Hill in London in the same year. Some thirty-six years later, Lord Henry Percy was also beheaded at Parliament Street in York. I wonder if anyone amongst the crowds that day noticed the phantom of a lady in a green dress carrying a bunch of blood-red roses for her former lover?

## *Micklegate Bar – Traitor's Gate*

*The Gate of Kings and Queens*

The rectangular gatehouse of Micklegate Bar marks the main entrance to the city from the south. It is also the traditional entry point for Kings and Queens visiting York. In a ceremony dating back to Richard II in 1389, monarchs stop at the bar and ask permission from the Lord Mayor of York to enter; they then must touch the State Sword before entering the city.

*How to Treat a Traitor*

Micklegate Bar for over 340 years was also the place where traitors' heads were displayed to deter rebellion. For those found guilty of treason, the punishment was indeed severe. Many were hung, drawn and quartered – or more correctly, drawn, hung and quartered – a fate that befell many of the sixteenth-century northern rebels. The tradition had endured from the fourteenth century, and a statute from those times describes in great detail the process which was used in this or a very similar form for centuries.

1. That the aforesaid…be drawn to the gallows.

(Dragged through the streets behind a horse.)

2. He is there to be hanged by the neck, and let down alive.

3. His bowels are to be taken out.

4. And if he be alive, to be burnt.

(For the half-choked man the sudden shock of seeing his insides removed before his eyes often ended the punishment earlier than intended.)

5. His head is to be cut off.

6. His body is to be divided into four parts.

7. And his head and quarters are to be placed where our King shall direct.

(The heads would go to Micklegate Bar, whilst other Yorkshire towns would compete for the remaining quarters to display on their walls or towers.)

*Words from the Bard*

Perhaps the most famous to have his head set upon a spike on Micklegate Bar was Richard, Duke of York, following the Battle of Wakefield in 1460. William Shakespeare immortalised the scene in Henry VI when Queen Margaret exclaims,:

'Off with his head, and set it on York gates/ So York may overlook the town of York.'

He was not the first to have his head chopped off to overlook the town of York, nor was he to be the last…

1403 Sir Henry Percy (Hotspur)
1405 Sir William Plumptom
1415 Lord Scrope
1461 Earl of Devon
1572 Earl of Northumberland
1663 Four of the Farnley Wood Conspirators
1746 William Conolly and James Mayne

*The overpowering feeling of being looked down upon from above, of staring eyes peering down on them from the darkness...*

*Hotspur, Hothead, No Head!*

In the fifteenth century the Percys were the most powerful family in Yorkshire.

In 1403 Sir Henry Percy, who was known as 'Hotspur' – because of his dashing riding skills and fiery nature – rebelled against King Henry IV. Harry Hotspur was defeated and killed at Shrewsbury and his head sent on to York and spiked on the Micklegate Bar as a warning to all rebellious Yorkshiremen. His body was buried in Whitchurch, but people said that 'Hotspur Lived', so he was dug up and his corpse displayed in Shrewsbury Market, then ground with salt between two millstones. His corpse was then hung, drawn and quartered. Finally his quarters were dispatched to London, Chester, Newcastle, and Bristol.

*The Long and the Short*

The severed heads were left on Micklegate Bar for long periods of time. It is recorded that James Mayne's head was illegally removed in 1754 – nine years after it had first been placed there. The record for the shortest stay on the Micklegate must go to Richard, Duke of York; his head only remained for three months. In 1461 his vengeful son, Edward IV, replaced his father's head with those of the Lancastrian leaders captured at the battle of Towton. The Earl of Devon was the most prominent of these leaders, and his head replaced Richard's on the spike!

*Tailor Gets Ahead*

The last heads to gaze down from the Micklegate Bar were those of William Conolly and James Mayne, placed there following the battle of Culloden in 1746. A further twenty-one of their slaughtered Jacobite comrades were buried behind the castle wall. The pair continued their lonely vigil for eight long years, until one cold January night in 1754 when they were secretly removed. The authorities were outraged and offered a reward of £10 for the capture of the perpetrator. Word reached the King, and he demanded to know who was responsible for this 'wicked, traitorous and outrageous proceeding'.

Some six months later William Arundel, a tailor, was convicted and sentenced to two years' imprisonment and if he failed to find £200 surety as to his good behaviour, two years more. It seems a strange that the tailor chose to steal a pair of heads – if William had been a hatter by trade it may have been easier to understand! Perhaps he was fortunate to catch the judge on a good day – otherwise his head may well have become the last incumbent of the Micklegate Bar.

*Eyes Still Watching?*

There have been a number of disturbing reports made by visitors to the city, with no prior knowledge of the previous gruesome history of Micklegate Bar, experiencing a strange phenomenon whilst in the area late at night. They all reported the overpowering feeling of being looked down upon from above,

*Hanged in chains from Clifford's Tower..*

of staring eyes peering down on them from the darkness above. Some who peered upwards into the darkness of the Bar reported seeing pairs of small glowing red lights eight or ten centimetres apart slowly swaying left and right. Others who dared not look upwards reported hurrying through the archway and feeling the sensation of drops of warm liquid falling down onto them from above, yet when they attempted to wipe it away their hands remained dry, and there were no marks or stains upon their clothing.

## *Clifford's Tower*

*Hanged in Chains from the Tower*

In the eleventh century York was recognised as one of the most important cities in England, it was an important base for holding and administering the North, and it was to become the site of two castles built by William the Conquer during the years immediately following his conquest. The principle castle was begun in 1068, as part of a campaign to subdue the resistance to Norman settlement in the North. It featured wooden defences atop a high conical mound overlooking the river Ouse. Within a year its defences were destroyed during violent local rebellions, but the Normans quickly rebuilt it after suppressing the rebels and taking harsh reprisals against the citizens of York.

Another wooden castle was built to replace the burned building, which survived until the thirteenth century when it was blown down by freak gales. A new castle constructed of stone was built in 1270 in a quatrefoil shape on the orders of Henry III. However, the roof of the tower was destroyed by fire in 1684.

In 1322, the tower gained its present name when Roger de Clifford was executed by Edward II for treason; Clifford was hanged in chains from the walls of the tower, and for ever after the building has been known as 'Clifford's Tower'.

*Crusades Against the Unbelievers*

The site of Clifford's Tower, the keep of York's medieval castle, still bears witness to one of the most horrifying events in the history of English Jewry. On the fateful night of 16 March 1190, the feast of 'Shabbat ha-Gadol', the small Jewish community of York was gathered together for protection inside the tower. These were difficult times – in the previous 100 years three major crusades had been waged by the Christian countries of Europe with the purpose of recapturing Palestine from the Mohammedans. The specific purpose of these religious wars was to free the Sepulchre of Jesus, sacred to the Christians, from the Moslem 'unbelievers'. In many cities in England anti-Semitic riots were commonplace; ignorant mobs were incited by the leaders of the crusades to pillage and massacre whole Jewish communities. A common cry was 'before attempting to revenge ourselves upon the Moslem unbelievers, let us first revenge ourselves upon the "killers of Christ" living in our midst!'

*Sanctuary in the Castle*

During the month of March 1190, tensions had risen in York and a number of the Jewish community had been murdered. The alarmed community with their leader Joseph sought shelter in the royal castle tower, where they were besieged by an angry mob. One day when the warden happened to be gone, the Jews became apprehensive that on his return he might hand them over to the besieging mob, and on his return they denied him admission. The angry warden called in the aid of the sheriff of the county, Richard Mabebys, a noble who happened to be deeply in debt to the Jewish money-lenders, and he took over command of the developing siege. Tensions continued to increase as a monk dressed in white robes celebrated Mass each morning in front of the tower, fanning the flames of anti-Semitism and hatred in the mob. A dislodged stone falling from the battlements of the tower struck the monk and killed him; his death infuriated the mob to a still higher degree, and they set fire to the tower.

*The Terrible Alternative*

The terrified hapless Jews were by now short of rations. Surrender to the angry besieging mob spelled forced baptism, possible rape of the women and children and death by torture for the men. In a final act of desperation large sums of money were offered for their safety, but these were rejected by the maddened rioters. In obedience to the exhortations of their religious leader, Yom Tob of Joigny, they chose the terrible alternative of laying hands upon themselves, in a scene reminiscent of the Siege of Massada in AD 70.

Each man first cut the throats of his own wife and children, then ten men were chosen by lot to kill the survivors. These remaining ten then drew lots to establish which among them would kill the other nine. The following day the burning citadel was captured, the few who were still alive were murdered by the mob, who then, led by Richard Mabebys, made their way to the cathedral where the records of the debts to the Jews were in safe keeping. Here they forced the guardians of the records to hand them over and they were burned in the sanctuary.

Today a plaque at the castle is an everlasting reminder of the terrible night in the history of the city when a small, frightened, but proud community chose to end their lives rather than betray their beliefs.

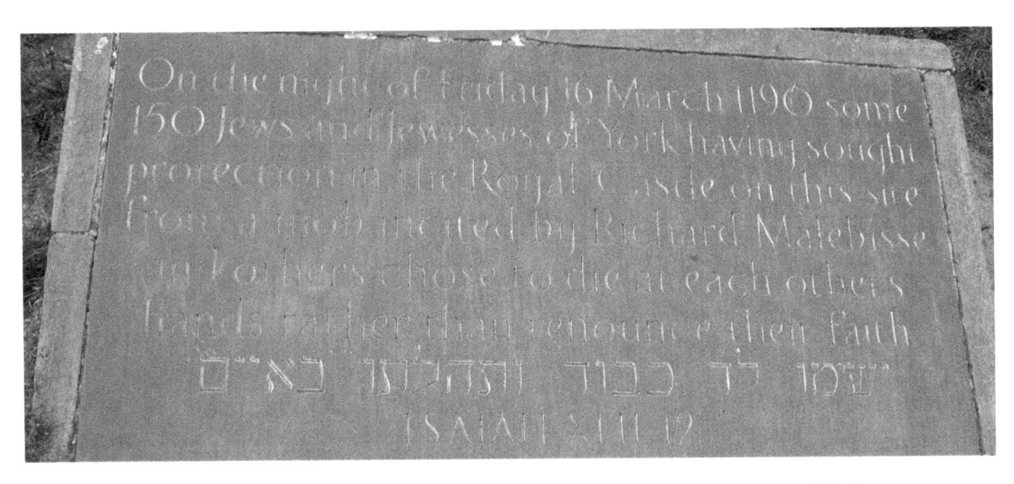


*A small, frightened, but proud community chose to end each other's lives rather than betray their beliefs.*

On the night of Friday 16 March 1190 some
150 Jews and Jewesses of York having sought
protection in the Royal Castle on this site
from a mob incited by Richard Malebisse
and others chose to die at each other's
hand rather than renounce their faith
ISAIAH XLII 12

*Walls Dripping Blood*

Today, over 800 later, strange manifestations are still witnessed at Clifford's Tower. Visitors, most often little girls, have reported seeing the gruesome phenomenon of blood pouring down the walls of this medieval fortification. Visible to everyone are the reddish stains on the gatehouse. Scientific tests have established that the red stains are caused by iron oxide in the stone, however none of the stone samples taken from the quarry close to Tadcaster which was used to construct the present tower have ever contained any trace of iron oxide.

## The Treasurer's House

*Threatened to Haunt the House!*

The post of Treasurer was created in the eleventh century by York's first Norman Archbishop, Thomas of Bayeux, after he discovered the Minster's affairs in disarray. It became the Treasurer's responsibility to manage the Minster – even in matters as mundane as keeping the altars supplied with candles – and to oversee repairs. The building we see today was built on the site of the original Treasurer's House, which was originally built over a Roman road. By the time the present building was built in the late sixteenth and early seventeenth centuries, it was a private residence. Frank Green, a wealthy local businessman, visionary and eccentric, owned the house from 1897. He not only renovated the house but also left his outstanding collection of antiques to the National Trust. He felt so passionately about the house that he even threatened to return to haunt the house if any of his furniture was ever moved after his death!

*Late Back from the Ball*

A number of phantoms allegedly haunt the house, one of them the ghost of George Aislaby, who met his untimely end as the result of a duel. He came from a wealthy family who owned Fountains Hall, and eventually purchased the Treasurer's House from Lord Fairfax. The family became well established in York society, and in January 1674, with Mary Mallorie, a co-heiress of Studley, they attended a high society ball held at the Duke of Buckingham's house in nearby Skeldergate. The ball continued late into the night, and the vivacious Miss Mallorie, enjoying herself, stayed on with the man to whom she was betrothed, Jonathan Jennings. A servant who had been dispatched to escort Miss Mallorie safely home failed to collect her, and it was decided that Jonathan would take the lady home in his own carriage. In the early hours of the morning upon reaching the Treasurer's House, repeated knockings failed to awake anyone, and it was decided that Mary would spend the night at the house of a relative of her fiancé.

*Frank Green, a wealthy local business man, felt so passionately about the Treasurer's House that he even threatened to return to haunt the residence if any of his furniture was ever moved after his death!*

*Honour Defended*

The following day believing that her virtue had been compromised, 'high words' passed between Jonathan Jennings and her brother-in-law George Aislaby, this led to a quarrel, the quarrel to a blow, and the blow led to a challenge. The following morning the duel was fought in nearby Penley Crofts, and the unfortunate George was mortally wounded defending the lady's honour, and was carried home by his second, to the Treasurer's House where he died by nightfall. Word of the death of his adversary reached a shocked Jonathan Jennings and fearing the repercussions he hastily borrowed a coach from his friend the Duke of Buckingham and hurried to London to obtain a pardon from Charles II.

*Final Twist to the Tale*

York society was shocked and scandalised by the whole affair. Later Jennings returned to York, though ironically in a final twist to the tale, Miss Mallorie, the original cause of the fateful quarrel, never married him, and indeed remained a spinster until her death a number of years later. George Aislaby was buried in the Minster, close to the choir screen, but it is claimed that his ghost still continues to haunt the Treasurer's House.

*Most Told Tale?*

Possibly one of the most recounted ghost stories in the whole of York is the series of events recorded by Harry Martindale in 1953. At the time extensive alterations were being carried out to the Treasurer's House, together with archaeological surveys. Young Harry, an apprentice aged around seventeen years, had been working in one of the cellars, installing piping for a new central heating system. On the day in question he was working alone down in the cellar, and was standing on a short ladder. When he first heard the sound of a trumpet, he paid little attention, other than the feeling of sight surprise that the sound of a brass band could have reached him deep

*He was carried home by his second, to the Treasurer's House where he died by nightfall.*

in the cellars below the house. The sound drew nearer and nearer, and suddenly the figure of a horse came through the solid stone cellar wall. He later described it as a large lumbering beast – its fetlocks heavy and shaggy like a great carthorse. Harry fell from his ladder to the earth floor in a state of shock and confusion, where he crouched in total disbelief as he stared at the scene which was unfolding before him. Astride the back of the horse was a man dressed in Roman costume, and following him were a group of soldiers, not marching in an orderly formation but stumbling and shuffling along in a dispirited fashion, with bowed heads. They took no notice of Harry as he lay in the spot where he had fallen on the cellar floor, but the details of their appearance were to remain clearly in his mind.

*Romans on their Knees*

He later described them as small in stature as well as shabby and unkempt in appearance. They wore rough home-made clothes and their sandals, cross-gated to the knees, were poorly made, and the coarse green tunics gave the impression that they had been roughly dyed. Each carried a round shield, a long spear and a short sword; the finest part of their attire appeared to be their helmets, complete with plumes of undyed feathers. He could not recollect any standard or banner, but clearly remembered the trumpet which he described as a long straight instrument, which appeared to have been much used and was worn and battered. The part of the cellar through which the dejected bunch of soldiers were passing was low and narrow, and some half a metre above the level of the old Roman road, the *Via Decumana*, which the archaeologists had recently uncovered, together with a fallen column from the headquarters building. At the time when Harry had first seen the horse coming through the wall, the group appeared to be without legs, but as they exited the other side of the cellar they were walking on the original level of the Roman road itself. The whole group passed slowly through the cellar, with an air of utter and complete dejection, and silently disappeared through the opposite wall.

*Shared Experience*

Shocked and trembling, Harry frantically scrambled up the cellar steps to the safety of the ground floor. Here he stumbled across the curator who, noticing his agitation said, 'you've seen the Roman soldiers, haven't you?' The remark was a great comfort to the ashen-faced youth, as he realised that he was not going out of his mind, and that other people had previously shared the same experience. The curator suggested that he write down exactly what he had seen, and he was later astonished to discover that two other people had also left accounts, giving identical details.

*First reported in the last century is the apparition of a phantom lurking in a quiet alleyway just off Coney Street.*

*Twenty-Year Secret*

For the next twenty years Harry was to keep quiet about his strange experience down in the cellars of the Treasurer's House; he only shared the events of that day with a few very close friends and it was not until 1974 that he could be persuaded to make public what had happened to him. Harry Martindale became PC Martindale, an honest and upright citizen who would never have dreamt of adding anything to his account that had not actually happened. Following his revelations he was questioned by many experts in Roman history, who were all impressed by the details he was able to give. An interesting fact which they were able to explain to Harry, and had always puzzled him was the shape of their shields. Harry clearly remembered the soldiers he saw were carrying round shields, and yet Romans are usually depicted with the rectangular curved Scutum used by Legionnaires. What is not commonly known is that round shields were often used by auxiliary troops during the fourth century. His descriptions of the Roman soldiers are far closer to the way historians now believe that they would have looked than the views presented by the glamorised Hollywood epics. The one question which Harry has asked throughout has been, 'Why me? I wasn't interested in either ghosts or Romans!'

## *Judges Court – off Coney Street*

*Dragging Footsteps*

First reported in the last century is the phantom which lurks in a quiet alleyway just off Coney Street. He has been described as a large man with dragging footsteps, and sightings were always accompanied by a strange tinkling sound. For many years he continued to be one of York's most active ghosts – he even appeared when a tour guide, who was showing a group of visitors around the city, paused for a while in Judges Court to describe a point of interest. Who the man may be, nobody seems to know for certain, but part of the mystery may have been solved a number of years ago when workmen were carrying out some renovation work in Judges Court. They discovered hidden in one of the old buildings a disused well shaft. Peering down the old well with the aid of a torch they were horrified to see a human skeleton at the bottom of the well. The bones were those of a large man, and though most of the clothing had decayed away to dust, it was clear that he was wearing a pair of fine leather riding boots, one of which had a broken spur. This was believed to explain the strange tinkling sound which accompanies the ghostly resident. Who the man was, and how he came to lie at the bottom of the well remains a mystery to this day.

# Chapter 3
# Haunted Pubs – Beers, Wines and Spirits?

*Early Pubs – in the Beginning*

As most early alehouses were private houses they were not regulated or licensed, but by the late fifteenth century some regulation was introduced for taxation purposes. Alehouse signs over the door, often originally a bush or branch, (hence 'Bull & Bush') were compulsory from 1477. This is why so many pub names go back to the War of the Roses ('Rose & Crown', 'White Hart', 'Blue Boar', etc.). In York in the Middle Ages it is said there was a monastery for every day of the week (seven), a church for every week of the year (fifty-two) and a pub for every day of the year (three hundred and sixty-five). This is not far wrong, as there were seven major monastic houses, about forty-five churches, and about two hundred inns and alehouses. When dating pubs, it is necessary to distinguish between the date of the building, which may be recent, and the date of licensing. So the Old Black Swan, Peasholme Green, and the Red Lion, Merchantgate, are old buildings of the fifteenth/sixteenth century, and as such are probably the oldest buildings in York functioning as pubs, but have only become pubs relatively recently; while the Golden Fleece, Pavement, has been licensed continuously since 1668, but was rebuilt in the nineteenth century. The oldest continuously licensed premises in York are believed to be:

1. Olde Starre, Stonegate – 1644
2. Golden Fleece, Pavement – 1668
3. Old White Swan, Goodramgate – 1703
4. Robin Hood (formerly Little John), Castlegate – 1733
5. Punch Bowl, Stonegate – 1761
6. Windmill, Blossom Street – 1770

## *The Black Swan – Peasholme Green*

This is a fine mid-sixteenth-century former merchant's mansion, possibly built by Sir Martin Bowes in 1560. Sir Henry Thompson, (Lord Mayor of York 1663 and 1672), extended it, and after the Red Lion, it is the oldest building functioning as a pub in York; though not licensed until the nineteenth century. The interior is mainly mid-seventeenth-century, with the best living rooms on either side of the front passage; the back bar was the original kitchen. A very fine staircase leads upstairs to the 'Trompe D'Oeil' room. This means 'deceiving the eye', and the room is so-called because the woodwork is painted to look like elaborate panelling. The house was the residence of the Bowes family in the fifteenth and sixteenth century. William Bowes, who was Sheriff in 1402 and Lord Mayor in 1417, owned it. His great-grandson was Sir Martyn Bowes. He eventually became Lord Mayor of London and goldsmith to Elizabeth I. He had a great love for York and presented to the city a Sword of State, which is still used to this day on ceremonial occasions.

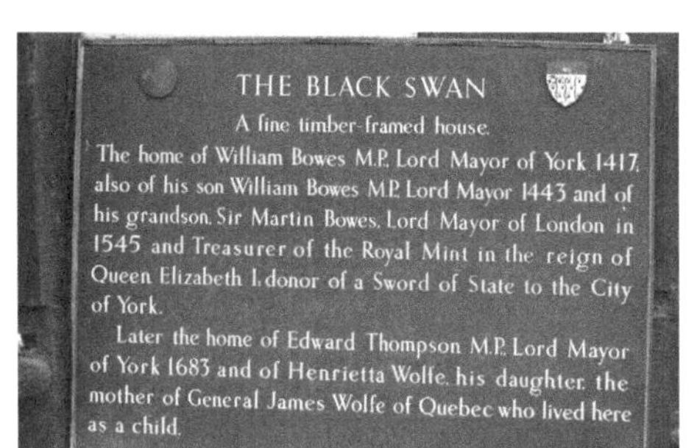


Above: *In the Black Swan stable yard alone there was stabling for around 100 horses.*

Left: *The Black Swan was one of York's major coaching inns.*

*From the Swan Came a Wolfe?*

The house later passed to the Thompson family, who also owned the Olde Starre Inne on Stonegate. Henry Thompson, who was Sheriff in 1601, was a wine merchant. Edward Thompson, born in 1670, had a country seat at the Old Hall, Long Marston and used this house on Peasholme Green as his town house. His daughter Henrietta Thompson married Colonel Edward Wolfe in 1724 at Long Marston. Thereafter the couple resided at the house here on Peasholme Green, but in July 1726 moved to Westerham, Kent, where James Wolfe was born on 2 January 1727. So James Wolfe was presumably conceived in York, perhaps in the Old Black Swan! As General Wolfe, he died taking Quebec from the French, and so laid the foundations of British Canada.

*Swan to Swan in Four Days!*

The Black Swan was one of York's major coaching inns. In 1706 on 12 April, the first stagecoach from London to York left the Black Swan, Holborn, for this inn, at 5 a.m. The journey from London to York took four days; on a 'good road' a stagecoach may have covered around 10 miles per hour (and in 1706 'good roads' were few and far between!) In 1786, the mail coaches first appeared, and by 1830 eighteen coaches left the Black Swan daily. By 1838, some 132 years since the first coaches travelled the road from London to York, the time for the journey was down to just twenty-one hours; a clear indication of the great improvements which had taken place in the road networks of England, the increasing numbers of coaching inns with changes of fresh horses, and the determination of the hard-working coachmen. Stagecoaches of the times included:

'Express' to Carlisle – Departed every Wednesday and Friday afternoon
'Tally Ho' to Carlisle – Departed Tuesday, Thursday and Saturday
'Rockingham' to Hull – Departed daily before noon
'Trafalgar' to Hull – Departed daily every afternoon
'Union' to Kendal – Departed daily every morning
'True Blue' to Leeds – Departed daily every afternoon

Many notables and well-known people of the times stayed here on visits to York, including Charles Dickens and the Brontë Sisters.

*An Old Flame?*
There are two ghosts who are claimed to haunt this old hostelry. The first and most often seen is the ghost of a young lady in a long white dress who stands quietly in the bar gazing intently at the fireplace. She is always described as having long flaxen hair, and she appears to glow slightly as if reflecting the flickering of the flames from the fire, although on many occasions she has been seen when no fire is actually burning in the grate. Despite her frequent appearances no one has ever seen her face, since she is always seen either staring down on to the flickering flames of the fire or sometimes gazing thoughtfully out of the window with her back turned to the living inhabitants of the pub.

*The Missed Appointment*
Encounters have also been reported with the ghost of a small workman of Victorian appearance wearing a bowler hat. He fidgets and tuts as if waiting for something or perhaps someone who is late for some pre-arranged appointment. He waits impatiently and sometimes checks the time on a pocket watch, which he frequently pulls from his waistcoat pocket. Eventually he just fades away into nothingness, only to return another day to wait once again for a meeting which it seems will never ever take place.

## *Red Lion – Merchantgate*

*Lion, Horse, Pig*
The Red Lion is built on thirteenth-century foundations, with fourteenth/fifteenth-century superstructure and it is on the corner nearest Fossgate/Merchantgate. It has a reputed thirteenth-century bread oven in the front bar, so it claims to be the oldest building used as a pub, though it has only been licensed since the nineteenth century. It was formerly behind the Black Horse, Fossgate, and they both served the old pig market on Foss Bridge. The tethering rings for the pigs are still visible on the bridge. On market days the stench and noise from the livestock as they were poked and prodded by the local butchers prior to being led away for slaughter must have been something to behold. On the first floor there is a priest's hole between two bedrooms, with access through the chimney. There is also a legend that Dick Turpin hid here and escaped through a window.

*The Red Lion claims to be the oldest building used as a pub, though it has only been licensed since the nineteenth century.*

*Meet the Real Dick Turpin*
This infamous highwayman has been immortalised in numerous books, at least three full-length films, and several TV series. According to legend, Dick Turpin once rode from London to York in a single day in order to establish an alibi for a stagecoach robbery. It was generally assumed at the time that nobody could be in London in the morning and in York by the evening of the same day. We now know that Turpin never made such a ride.

*Swift Nick*
It is believed that the feat was in fact achieved, if at all, by another notorious highwayman, John Nevison on his trusty steed 'Black Bess', in 1668, over thirty years before Dick Turpin was even born. Following his ride Nevison was to become known as 'Swift Nick'.

Dick Turpin was born in 1705 in Hempstead near Saffron Walden, Essex, where he went to school. He later trained as a butcher, and sold meat stolen at night by local rustlers. In 1734 he joined the Gregory Gang, a vicious band of house-breakers who tortured householders into revealing the whereabouts of their valuables. The reign of terror was to be short-lived, and most of the notorious Gregory Gang were caught and hanged within a year.

In 1737, Turpin set up with another outlaw, Tom King, as highwaymen in Epping Forest. In an ambush by the authorities at Whitechapel, Turpin accidentally shot Tom King, and in the ensuing chaos he made his escape.

*John Palmer alias Dick Turpin*
He eventually moved north, and to avoid detection changed his name to John Palmer. He settled at the Ferry House Inn, Brough, and became a horse 'dealer', and made a handsome living selling stolen horses.

On 2 October 1738, he shot a cock in the Main Street of Brough, and then in an argument which followed, threatened to shoot a local innkeeper who complained. The village constable became involved, and Turpin was detained. He was committed to trial at Beverley, then York for breach of peace.

Soon after he was taken into custody, the local authorities made enquiries as to how exactly 'John Palmer' had made his money, and inevitably the constables learned of several outstanding complaints made against 'John Palmer' for sheep and horse stealing in nearby Lincolnshire. Thus, 'Palmer' was transferred to the cells of York Castle Prison (now part of the York Castle Museum).

*There is also a legend that Dick Turpin hid here and escaped through a window.*

*Life Turns on a Sixpence*

From his cell, Turpin wrote to a family member who still resided in Essex, close to Turpin's birthplace. The letter was a plea for help; requesting his brother-in-law to 'procure an evidence from London that could give me a character that would go a great way towards my being acquitted'. In reality the letter was a thinly disguised request for his brother-in-law to provide him with an alibi.

The plan might have worked, but it backfired. Turpin's brother-in-law refused to pay the sixpence postage demanded for what he believed was probably the eighteenth-century equivalent of unsolicited mail, and as such, the letter was never delivered to him. This unpaid sixpence would prove the price of Turpin's life! The unread letter eventually fell into the hands of John Smith, the village postmaster, who was also the village schoolmaster, who had, years earlier, taught Turpin to read and write.

*The Schoolmaster's Reward*

Smith immediately recognised the distinctive handwriting of his former pupil, and travelled to York to consult with the magistrate and to identify 'John Palmer' as Dick Turpin. His former friend and mentor would later collect a handsome £200 reward for identifying the notorious highwayman to the authorities. On 22 March, Dick Turpin was tried for horse stealing, and sentenced to death at York's Knavesmire Gallows.

*The Three-Legged Mare*

First completed in 1379, Knavesmire was given a name synonymous with executions in London since the thirteenth century – Tyburn. The very name became feared throughout the land as many a thief, rogue, villain and murderer ended his days suspended from the Three-Legged Mare, as the tri-cornered scaffold became known – a great structure that could support up to twenty dangling corpses on busy execution days.

From as early as 1530, race meetings have been held at Knavesmire, and from 1708 on a regular basis, and from then onwards executions would be timed to coincide with race days, creating great festivals of sport and death; bawdy, brawling, excited crowds would fill their day with both, and for a small fee they enjoyed the twin spectacles from John Carr's great grandstand (built in 1754), from which ten thousand were guaranteed the best view in York.

On some occasions, when the condemned man had finished his dance of death at the end of the hemp, he would be cut down and paraded through the streets for the further amusement of the bawdy crowd. Medical men – knives and saws at the ready – would often attend public hangings, awaiting the time when the crowd became bored with events, and they could seize the corpse.

It was permitted by law for them to butcher the recently executed on their dissection tables, for the purpose of anatomical research – hardly a pleasant thought for the condemned man or his family as they made their way to the Knavesmire on execution day!

*Hang Them All*

During the Tudor reign less than fifty offences carried the death penalty, but by the 1820 there were over two hundred. A barrister by the name of Charles Phillips, who served as a commissioner in the Court of Insolvent Debtors, wrote in 1856: 'we hanged for anything – for a shilling – for five pounds – for cattle – for coining – for forgery, even witchcraft – for things that were and things that could not be'.

Pleas from Turpin's father to have the sentence commuted to transportation fell on deaf ears. His father had himself been cleared just a few days earlier at the Essex Assizes of horse stealing, one of Turpin's stolen horses having been found at his alehouse.

Following his sentence, whilst awaiting execution, numerous visitors frequented Turpin's cell as he enjoyed his new, but brief celebrity. As the day of his execution drew closer the flamboyant rogue was resolved to meet his death with dignity and calm. He spent the remainder of his money on fine new clothes and handmade leather shoes, to look his best on his last day, and even hired five mourners for ten shillings each.

*My Old Friend the Hangman*

On 7 April 1739, the day of his execution, Dick Turpin rode through the streets of York in an open cart, being theatrical and bowing to the gawking crowds. At York's Knavesmire Gallows he climbed the ladder to the gibbet, and then sat for half an hour addressing the assembled crowd in the manner of an entertainer, chatting to the guards, and to his executioner.

Public hangings were always a good excuse for an unofficial public holiday: the excited crowds would gather at the prison to follow the procession of the condemned men from their cells to the gallows; and having seen their souls strengthened, and tongues loosened, by various landlords along the route, would look forward to some participation. A full confession was always popular, both with the crowd and the authorities. It offered those who had sent the man to his death some vindication of their decision, and for the crowds, a salacious confession was considered fine entertainment.

Turpin offered no confession, but entertained the crowd with playful banter, cursing and weeping, and finally he regaled his attentive audience with a long and rousing farewell speech. Ironically, the hangman on that April day was Thomas Hadfield, once Turpin's friend and a former Gregory Gang member, who had earlier been pardoned because he had agreed to become a hangman. In a final grand gesture Turpin pulled from his waistcoat pocket a fine carved ivory whistle, and offered it to his executioner as a souvenir of the day. Perhaps he intended that it should be passed on to John Smith – after all by, 'blowing the whistle' on his former pupil he was now £200 richer!

*Cause of Death – Suicide*

An account of Turpin's execution in the *York Courant* on the 7 April 1739 notes his brashness even at the end, 'with undaunted courage [he] looked about him, and after speaking a few words to the topsman, he threw himself off the ladder and expired in about five minutes'.

Possibly in death at least, the flamboyant rogue, Dick Turpin, attained some of the gallantry that had eluded him throughout his life. Despite the fame of his hanging, because he threw himself from the ladder before his executioner Thomas Hadfield could perform the execution, Turpin's death in fact was technically a suicide.

*Dick Turpin was transferred to the cells of York Castle Prison (now part of the York Castle Museum).*

*The Entertainment Continues*

The entertainment for the crowd continued long after the last gasping breath of the condemned man. Before the blood set in his arteries, the ink had dried on the page of one of the chapbooks, sold by the many hawkers who frequented the Knavesmire, along with the ballad sellers. For less than a penny a time they told the felon's tale in a manner guaranteed to enthral, with scant regard for the facts of the case. So the legends began; the exaggerated, romanticised, half-truths that would be re-told and added to in every alehouse and inn for the rest of time.

Once the horse racing was over, and the bawdy, excited crowds moved back into the city, the day's events would be re-enacted for money in many of the alehouse yards, by groups of actors. The most popular of these were attended by the hangman and his associates, who would sometimes have on offer tempting souvenirs taken from the condemned man, after his removal from the gallows, for the more ghoulish members of the crowd to purchase.

The landlords who had earlier in the day strengthened the condemned man on his way to the gallows would receive their reward as the revellers filled their inns, and drank late into the night, retelling their account of the death of a legend.

*Body Snatchers*

Turpin was said to have been buried in the churchyard of St George's church, York. However, a short time after the burial his corpse was dug up and stolen by body snatchers working for anatomists, but it appears to have been subsequently recovered and reburied in the same place, this time with the addition of quicklime to destroy the remains more rapidly. As an account from the times explained: 'The corpse was brought to The Blue Bear in Castlegate where it

*Turpin was buried in the churchyard of St George's church. A headstone in the churchyard commemorates him, but is not at the precise location, which to this day remains undiscovered.*

lay in state until the next morning. The grave in St George's churchyard was dug remarkably deep, and the people who acted as mourners took such measures as thought would secure the body, yet about three o' clock on the following morning, some persons were observed in the churchyard who carried it off. The populace, having an intimation where it had been conveyed, found it at the back of Stonegate, in the garden of one of the surgeons of the city. Hereupon they took the body, laid it on a board, covered it with straw, and having carried it through the streets in a kind of triumphal manner, they filled the coffin with unslacked lime, and buried it in the grave where it had been before deposited.' A headstone in the churchyard commemorates him, but is not at the precise location, which to this day remains undiscovered.

*Ghost of Galloping Horsemen*

Over the years there have been a number of sightings, on dark, misty, moonless winter's nights of the phantoms of two horsemen galloping at breakneck speed through the deserted streets of York. The second chasing figure is reported as wearing a long frock coat and tri-cornered hat, and riding a large black horse. I wonder if the phantoms may be of Dick Turpin chasing his brother-in-law, who all those years ago cost the highwayman his life for the sake of a sixpenny letter?

## *The York Arms – High Petergate*

*Tormented in the Toilet!*

A mischievous sprightly female spook has scared many a guest in the gents' toilet here by suddenly appearing and disappearing. Her identity is unknown, but it has been suggested that she may be the same ghost who haunts the Theatre Royal nearby, known by some as the Grey Lady.

*The York Arms – a mischievous sprightly female spook has scared many a guest in the gents' toilet here. The inn is also the haunt of a poltergeist that annoyingly locks doors, throws cutlery and kitchen equipment around and generally makes a nuisance of itself.*

She has sometimes been described as a white or grey blur, which some say resembles an old or perhaps veiled lady, though a medium who visited the pub a number of years ago claimed that the ghost was of a playful child. On one occasion a former landlord became so frustrated by the mischievous ghost whilst redecorating the toilets that in a fit of rage he threw a loaded paint brush at it. The assault produced no effect; the missile passed through the ghost leaving a paint smear on the wall.

*Bath-Time Intrusions*

The inn is also the haunt of a poltergeist that annoyingly locks doors, throws cutlery and kitchen equipment around and generally makes a nuisance of itself. An old pair of bellows once unhooked themselves from the wall, rose up to avoid an ornamental plate, and glided lazily to the ground several yards away. Doors have been opened and closed by unseen hands (a draught might just manage to open a very stiff door, but would it be polite enough to hastily close it again, upon discovering the startled landlord in his bath?)

The most recent manifestation occurred in an upstairs bedroom, where a small ornament on a windowsill seemed to fascinate the ghost. Over and over again the ornament slid up and down the length of the sill, with almost hypnotic power. The casement window was finally slammed shut, followed by a family portrait being sent crashing to the ground.

## *The Snickleway Inn, formerly The Anglers Arms – Goodramgate*

*Haunting Fragrance*

On the top floor of this small cosy pub is possibly the most elusive spirit in York. It never betrays its presence by even the tiniest of sounds. Nor has it ever been seen, yet its presence is always easy to detect, since the strong and distinctive fragrance of lavender will waft through the rooms, only to dissipate as suddenly and mysteriously as it first filled the air.

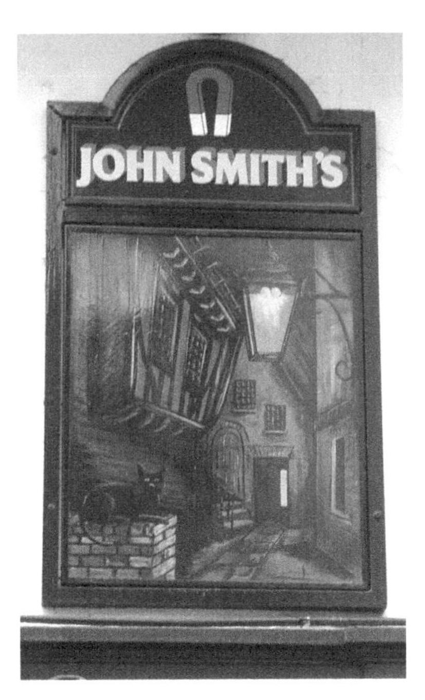


*On the top floor of this small cosy pub is possibly the most elusive spirit in York. The most tangible of all the spirits who haunt the Snickleway Inn seems to be a creature of great age, intelligence and utter evil.*

*Child on the Stairs*

On the stairs around the middle floor has been seen the ghost of a friendly Victorian child. At one time the pub cat enjoyed playing with this invisible partner, and was often seen purring round the feet of an unseen figure. One old man who visited the pub said that many years ago the ghost of the Victorian child could often be seen sitting on the stairs, looking down at the more solid pub inhabitants below. The story most associated with the little figure is that she was a particularly lively girl who one day ran down the pub staircase and out of the front door into the bustling street outside – straight into the path of a horse-drawn brewer's dray. Yet despite her painful death beneath the hooves of the dray horses her presence is always said to feel friendly or playful.

*Something in the Cellar*

Down in the dark cellars below the pub however lurks a third ghost – one who is neither friendly nor playful. The only entrance to the cellar is through a trap door behind the bar, which for safety reasons is kept firmly locked, yet suddenly and frequently the gas taps, which pump the beer from the cellar to the bar above, are turned off. The taps in the dark empty cellar are always turned off so forcibly by the invisible spirit that the landlady requires a cloth to wrap around the tap head before it can be turned on again. This presence in the cellar is the most tangible of all the spirits who haunt the Snickleway Inn and seems to be a creature of great age, intelligence and utter evil. In past times neither the playful pub cat nor the pub dog could ever be enticed to venture down into the cellar, and past landladies and landlords have admitted that when the regulars have all gone home and the pub is empty and dark, late at night, they would never ever venture down into the darkness.

*Ignorance and Superstition*
In the grim days of the seventeenth century, York was still plagued by superstition and fear of the unknown. In those times physical defects were often regarded as 'marks of the devil' or punishment from God.

Born into this often sad and ignorant world in 1697 was a young man by the name of Marmaduke Buckle. He was born into a wealthy family, but sadly born crippled. As he grew up he became more and more isolated by his illness, and every day faced ignorance and superstition, as he was persecuted by his contemporaries.

*Daily Torment*
As the years passed, his daily torment drove him to retreat to an upstairs room, where he would spend his lonely hours in isolation, sadly gazing down from his window onto the bustling street of Goodramgate below. His isolation continued, and eventually loneliness and depression drove him to suicide, and he hanged himself from a central roof beam in his room. Possibly his last act before taking his own life was to scratch his name in the plaster wall of his room. Below his name are recorded the brief dates of his sad life.

Marmaduke Buckle
1715
1697
.......

17

*Eyes Watching*
Poor Marmaduke Buckle is not a vindictive ghost. His presence is betrayed only by a feeling of the deep sadness and rejection which he suffered during his brief life. Sometimes visitors to the inn tell of the sound of a door opening, or the lighting of a lamp in an empty room; or very rarely the feeling of being watched by the same sad young eyes that gazed down onto Goodramgate from his window almost 300 years earlier.

## *The Cock & Bottle – Skeldergate*

*Saucy Spirit*
George Villers, the second Duke of Buckingham, who lived during the reign of Charles II, is the saucy spirit who is claimed to haunt the public house, on the site of his former mansion on Skeldergate. Villers was made immortally infamous, as the hero of the nursery rhyme 'Georgy Porgie' which refers to his downfall in Parliament in 1673. Since the first reports in the 1970s numerous pub customers have reported sightings of the ghost. His ghost makes its presence known mostly to women and has been described as a 'shadowy figure with long black curly hair and embroidered clothing'.

During his lifetime the Duke spent a great deal of time trying to turn base metal into gold, without much success. Villers was known in his day as a wit, poet and politician during the reign of Charles II. His scandalous lifestyle and numerous affairs outraged society and surpassed even those of his sovereign. He owned estates in Yorkshire and died in the county in 1687. It is recorded that he wished to be buried in York, but his wishes were ignored and he was buried in Westminster Abbey.

*The ghost at the Cock & Bottle most certainly has a taste for female company and on some occasions has been known to stroke and even fondle young ladies. The pub is also subjected to sudden unnatural cold spells when the temperature plummets dramatically.*

*The Groping Ghost!*

On one occasion the ghost was caught spying on a former landlady whilst she took a shower soon after taking over the pub. Through the frosted glass of the shower she saw a large man, with long black curly hair, walk into the bathroom and peer through the glass into the shower, after a few seconds the man left and she heard his footsteps climbing upstairs towards the attic. The woman's startled cries brought her husband running and together they searched the upper floors. No sign of the man could be found.

The ghost most certainly has a taste for female company and on some occasions has been known to stroke and even fondle young ladies. On other occasions a stone at the back of the fireplace was said to glow more brightly than the fire itself. Other customers have reported a shadowy figure sitting alone at a table, who has then been seen to dissolve into thin air.

*Chilly Gloom*

The pub is also subjected to sudden unnatural cold spells when the temperature plummets dramatically, an atmosphere of gloom pervading the normally lively pub. In past times poltergeist activity was often reported; doors opened and closed by themselves, small articles were moved around the pub by unseen hands and people reported having an eerie feeling of being watched by hostile invisible eyes.

*The Punch Bowl was rumoured to be a house of ill repute in times gone by. A desperate spirit is said to re-enact her last moments at the Punch Bowl, still running from room to room, trying to evade her drunken assailant.*

## *The Punch Bowl – Stonegate*

*Liberals, Horse Fanciers and Campanologists*

Rebuilt in 1931, this inn goes back to 1675 as a coffeehouse. It was a meeting place for the Whigs (a political party and the origin of the Liberals) who drank punch, hence its name. The Tories of the times preferred port and red wines. It has been licensed continuously since 1761, so it is the fifth oldest pub in York. It was also the headquarters of the York Race Committee and the resort of York Minster bell-ringers in the eighteenth century.

Another hostelry in York believed to be frequented by two ghosts, the inn was rumoured to be a house of ill repute in times gone by. The first ghost dates from more recent times and is said to be that of a nineteenth-century landlord who perished in a fire.

*Murder in the Whorehouse*

The second is a reminder of the building's more colourful past. Legend has it that on a bitter winter's night a man seeking female company called at the house. After imbibing copious amounts of alcohol, he began to harass a young girl, an innocent flower seller who had called at the inn hoping to make some sales on her way home. She rejected his advances. In a drunken rage he pursued the terrified girl around the inn, finally cornering her in an upstairs room where he strangled her. Her desperate spirit is said to re-enact her last moments, still running from room to room, trying to evade her drunken assailant.

## *The Old White Swan – Goodramgate*

*Double Rates*

The Old White Swan is part timber-framed, but mainly brick. The centre ranges from the sixteenth century, set back from the street, with side wings from the mid-eighteenth century. The frontage to Goodramgate was rebuilt in 1771. It was recorded as an inn in 1703 – the third oldest continuously licensed pub in York. Various parts of it at various times have been a pigsty, a barber's shop, and a barn. The Gallery and Minstrel Bar show fine examples of timber framing and a former hayloft. The inn was in two parishes – Holy Trinity Kings Court, and Holy Trinity, Goodramgate – and so had to pay two sets of rates. Over the years this caused many disputes, and in the early seventeenth century a white line was painted through the courtyard and in through the kitchen door to show the boundary. In 1723 there was much searching for Papists and it was recorded that the parish constables spent one pound on ales whilst watching for Papists at night at the Swan! It was a major coaching and posting inn in the late eighteenth and early nineteenth centuries. In pre-railway days, it was much frequented by farmers and poultry dealers, who used to collect poultry around country districts surrounding York, and come to the Old White Swan to sell them at fixed times to their city clients, butchers and innkeepers.

*Papist Meeting Place*

A group of friendly spirits frequents this timber-framed establishment that is made up of an eclectic mix of no less than nine different buildings. Speculation has it that in times gone by the inn was a secret meeting place for Papists planning their escape to France, which may explain why furniture, and in particular chairs, are often found rearranged in a circle overnight. A former landlord of the inn is on record as saying that in a room closed to the public, furniture would whirl around in the air before crashing down in a large heap in the centre of the room. Further accounts talk of muffled voices, footsteps and a fire, which relights itself.

*The Old White Swan – various parts of this pub at various times have been a pigsty, a barber's shop, and a barn. Furniture would whirl around in the air before crashing down in a large heap in the centre of the room.*

*The Old White Swan was a major coaching and posting inn in the late eighteenth and early nineteenth centuries.*

## *Site of the Old George Inn – Coney Street*

*Don't lose your head!*

Now under Leak & Thorp Department Store (now Next), only part of the gateway and pillar to the original coaching yard survives, as it was demolished in 1868. It was originally medieval merchants' mansion of the fifteenth century, maybe near the site of the Bull (later 'the Rose'), which was owned by the Mayor and Corporation. In 1459 it was, 'ordained that from this day forth, no aliens coming from foreign parts, shall be lodged within the said city, liberties or suburbs thereof, but only in the Inn of the Mayor and Commonalty, at the sign of the Bull in Conying Street'.

The George first appears under Thomas Kaye, Sheriff of York in 1614. It had a large galleried quadrangle, and a fantastically decorated frontage with elaborate moldings. It was a major coaching inn in the eighteenth century and early nineteenth century, and many notables stayed here including Vanbrugh. One can imagine coaches tearing along Coney Street and turning sharply into the narrow entrance. When passengers on the roof complained that they had nearly had their heads knocked off, the coachman would say 'don't worry – there was over an inch to spare!'

*Final Journey*

There are accounts of sounds heard late at night in this part of the city of the clattering of horses' hooves, and the rattling and creaking of the iron-rimmed wheels of a mystery stagecoach, and the crack of the driver's whip, followed by the screech of the lurching coach as it once again

*Their dying screams are still said to ring around the empty rooms of the Olde Starre Inn in the dead of night.*

turns sharply down the narrow entrance yard. The final sounds heard are the screams of the rooftop passengers as once more they almost lose their heads and the sounds echo away down the alleyway into the silence and the dark.

## *The Olde Starre Inn – Stonegate*

*Starre of the Circus*

The oldest continuously licensed premises is in York, dating back to at least 1644, with a building of an even earlier date, so it may go back to the mid-sixteenth century. The earliest reference is of a printer, Thomas Broad, dwelling at Mistress Roger's house in Stonegate, over against the Starre in 1644. The Starre may be a reference to the Star of Bethlehem, guiding travellers to the Minster (and pub!) or to the crest of the innkeeper's company which is a sixteen-pointed star. The main block at the back of the yard is mid-sixteenth-century; the left-hand block is from around 1600. Originally there was a coaching yard in front but with the coming of the railways in 1840 this became redundant, and the yard was filled in with a shop fronting – Stonegate, hence the long passage to the pub. The Starre had stabling behind leading to Lop Lane (now Duncombe Place) and this was also used for circus animals and theatrical parties from the nearby Theatre Royal; so the pub was a popular resort for actors and entertainers. The first recorded landlord in 1644 was a staunch Royalist, and as the city fell to Parliament that year he was no doubt none too pleased to have to serve the despised Roundheads at his inn. The pub was sold for £250 in 1662, and in 1683 it was inherited by Edward Thompson, grandfather of General Wolfe, who also owned the house that is now the Old Black Swan, Peasholme Green. In 1733 to advertise the pub the landlord Thomas Bulman erected a sign across the road. He made a written agreement with John Moore, a shoemaker, and George Ambler, a saddler, that he could fix his sign to their premises across Stonegate; he was to pay them five pounds each at Candlemas, but they had to spent it in his company (i.e. in his pub!)

*Wounded Soldiers*

This inn has several different ghostly tales attached to it. It is claimed that the cellars date back to the tenth century, and that they were used to house and shelter wounded Royalist soldiers who had fought at the battle of nearby Marston Moor. Their dying screams are still said to ring around the empty rooms of the building in the dead of night. There is also the spirit of an old lady who has been glimpsed climbing the stair late at night, although this is one of a number of York ghosts who has only ever been seen by children.

*Fiendish Felines*

Visitors of a canine variety are often uneasy when taken inside the Olde Starre Inn; they often snarl and bristle with hostility as their eyes follow an invisible visitor around the room. One bold dog knocked itself unconscious when suddenly and unaccountably it leapt forwards and slammed into a wall. It seems they are most likely to sense the ghosts of two black cats who are said to haunt the building after being bricked up alive in the pillar between the door and the main bar many years ago during alterations to the building.

## *The Golden Fleece Inn – Pavement*

*Mint Your Own Money*

The second oldest continuously licensed premises in York, dating back to 1668, the Golden Fleece Inn takes its name from the wool trade, the staple trade of York from the thirteenth to the seventeenth century. The frontage is mid-nineteenth-century, but rear parts go back to the sixteenth century, and are relics of a courtyard for coaches. The Golden Fleece was a major coaching inn in the eighteenth and early nineteenth centuries. The jetty of Thomas Herbert's house and Lady Peckett's yard projects into the side passage. In 1667, Richard Booth, a York merchant was allowed to mint his own copper halfpennies, which are shown as having been produced 'at the Golden Fleece'.

*Lady Alice Peckett Walks Again*

Claimed to be amongst the oldest and most haunted of the coaching inns in York, it is mentioned in the York archives as far back as 1503, and before 1570 initially belonged to the Merchant Adventurers, who were responsible for the burgeoning woollen trade based on the river Ouse. The yard at the rear is named after Lady Alice Peckett, whose husband John was a one-time Lord Mayor of York and also owned this historic inn around 1702. Many guests have reported seeing the late Lady Peckett wandering the endless corridors and staircases of the Golden Fleece in the small hours. Including ghostly apparitions and moving furniture, hers is just one of the five supposed resident spirits at the Golden Fleece, most of whom seem to have taken up residence around the eighteenth century.

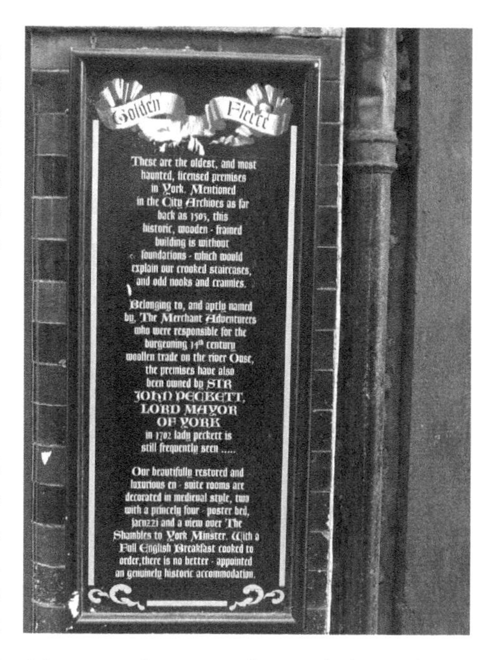


*Many guests have reported seeing the late Lady Peckett wandering the endless corridors and staircases of the Golden Fleece in the small hours.*

*Just one of the five supposed resident spirits at the Golden Fleece, most of whom seem to have taken up residence around the eighteenth century.*

*There have been occasions when visitors have fled in terror and refused to go back.*

## *The Roman Bath – St Sampson's Square*

*Sounds from the Bath*

There have been many instances of ghostly occurrences in the Roman baths below the pub with the same name. Inside the pub is one of the most novel, interesting and ancient display features to be found in any pub in the land: literally a Roman bath! Not a single or even double-sized bath, but large enough for a whole group of bathers, a great stone-built installation, the father of all modern saunas and Turkish baths, built by the Romans over 1,900 years ago. Whilst you enjoy a refreshing drink at your table, you are able to look down into the amazing floodlit excavation. At first it appears that the bath is ahead of you – until you realise that, thanks to the ingenious use of mirrors, what you see is actually underneath you.

*The Ghosts Within*

The manifestations of the majority of these spirits have been in the form of sounds rather than sightings. Most commonly footsteps can be heard when no one is around. Visitors also report the sound of water splashing as though someone were washing themselves. There have been occasions when visitors have fled in terror and refused to go back down, convinced that something has brushed against them. More recently during refurbishment of the entrance in the pub, which for obvious reasons took place at night, the decorator who was painting the walls at the bottom of the staircase refused to continue. He said, 'something was there'. The wall was only completed when a slightly braver painter was found, but even he would only work during daylight hours!

*Strange Lights in the Bathhouse*

The only alleged sighting so far took place approximately twelve years ago. Two men were spending the night in the Roman baths in order to raise money for a local charity. Both saw the exact same thing as they were settling down. A blinding light filled the room and the shape of a figure could be made out, the light disappeared as quickly as it had come, fading into the area where the bottom of the baths' cold-room (the Fridgearium) can be seen. The light was seen again by one of the men a couple of weeks later reflected in the mirrors that used to be fixed to the wall. Again it faded as though it were being sucked into a hole, at the same spot. The second man at the time was manager of the Roman baths and had been for some time. After the second sighting he packed his bags and left his employment without serving notice, and was not seen in York again!

*After the second sighting the manager packed his bags and left his employment at the Roman baths without serving notice, and was not seen in York again!*

## *Five Lions – Walmgate*

As with many old inns in York, The Five Lions has been largely rebuilt. Originally there was an additional floor which contained a long narrow apartment. This room had an earth floor and a barred gate leading to it – curious features which are claimed to have existed from the times when cock-fights were held here.

*Battle to the Death*

Cock-fighting was a popular sport with many seventeenth-century spectators, mainly due to the fact that it was a sport that cut across social classes. Most of the more publicised fights were organised for gentlemen by gentlemen. Large amounts of money would often be wagered on the outcome of each fight. However, common people were also very enthusiastic participants. Most of the fights were held in an inn, which was specially prepared, or in a cockpit. A cockpit was similar to an amphitheatre only smaller. The birds were matched by weight. Their beaks were filed down and their wings were clipped. Each cock was also outfitted with spurs which birds used as their major tool of aggression. A cock could be severely injured or mortally wounded as a result of the deep wounds inflicted by the spurs. Individual pairings were the most common types of cock-fighting; however, there were fights that involved large numbers of cocks. As many as thirty-two cocks would be put into a cockpit at one time. Few of the cocks survived this type of competition!

*I am sure that whilst in York that Squire Cunliffe could not resist visiting The Five Lions to enjoy what became his favourite sport – cock-fighting.*

*The Squire's Bedside Entertainment*

We know that the Brontës visited York, and I also know that in earlier times a neighbour of theirs, Squire Henry Owen Cunliffe of Wycoller Hall (1752-1818), had cause to visit the capital of the North in the year 1788, in order to defend himself in court against a claim of land on the Wycoller boundary. I am sure that whilst in York he could not resist visiting many of the inns to enjoy what became his favourite sport – cock-fighting. He considered it a noble sport, so much so that he even enjoyed it on his deathbed! A fairly obvious reference to him appears in Mrs Gaskell's *The Life of Charlotte Brontë*:

> Another Squire, of a more distinguished family and larger property – one is then led to imagine of better education but that does not always follow – died at his house, not many miles from Haworth, only a few years ago. His great amusement and occupation had been cock-fighting. When he was confined to his chamber with what he knew would be his last illness, he had cocks brought up there, and watched the bloody battle from his bed. As his mortal disease increased, and it became impossible for him to turn so as to follow the combat, he had looking glasses arranged in such a manner around and above him, as he lay, that he could still see the cocks fighting. And in this manner he died.

An interesting painting by Lanslett John Pott, RA, portraying an eighteenth-century gentleman and his friends holding a cock-fighting meeting indoors and entitled 'The Ruling Passion', is popularly associated with Squire Cunliffe.

*The Squire's Ghost Rediscovered*

In his book *Through Sorrow's Gates,* writer Halliwell Sutcliffe describes an encounter with the old Squire when one of his characters Ned O' Bracken stumbles across him, after a meal at a nearby inn, as darkness falls...

*With a sudden effort he pushed the door wide open and looked within, holding his breath for dread of the unknown whose secret he must learn.*

'A main, a main! My bird against yours for a sovereign,' were the first words he heard.

Now, a cock-fight was no new thing to Ned, but what in another place would have seemed usual enough was the cause of cringing dread to the man tonight ... Ned O' Bracken recalled the tale of another of the wild Cunliffe breed – how the Squire of that day lay a-dying, and called for a pair of fighting cocks, and died cheering the winning bird.

How if his ghost had come back to old scenes, old occupations? The hall had been untenanted and shunned for years; none would enter it for a cock-fight now, unless he was mad drunk or disembodied.

Again the shouts came from the upper chamber and Ned, drawn by an awful fascination, passed through the gate, and in between the straight, tall hollies that guarded each side of the doorway, and up the worn stone stairs. He moved more slowly and reluctantly with every step, and yet he felt compelled to mount. At last he stood upon the landing, in front of the closed door from under which light was stealing. With a sudden effort he pushed the door wide open and looked within, holding his breath for dread of the unknown whose secret he must learn.

What he saw was a company of twelve, surrounding the bodies of two fighting-cocks, one bird was dead, the other dying in its hour of victory. The men's faces were fierce and eager, and they were shouting wildly or cursing, according to the wagers they had made.

Squat, round-bellied bottles stood on the window seat, and in the neck of such bottles as were empty were thrust candles which had guided Ned into the midst of this harsh revelry. ...Now the candle flames, and now the lightning, revealed the dead bodies of the fighting-cocks, the bottles, some upright, some lying on their sides; revealed the wild faces of the revellers; revealed last of all the dark stain upon the floor which was connected with one of the far off Cunliffe tragedies...

A roar of thunder, then a crash of masonry as the chimney stack fell inward, filling the chamber with the odour of damp earth and soot. The wind got up again and howled; and then again it shrieked in agony, and swept through the hall door, left open by Ned on his first coming, and ran like a mad thing up the stair. The Squireen's mug fell to the floor. 'By the Heart, it's the Riding Squire himself!' he yelled, and raced wildly for the stair.

# Chapter 4
# Haunted Churches

## *St Michael-le-Belfry church*

The church is believed to take its name from its close proximity to the south-west tower of the Minster, which houses the Minster's peal of twelve bells. Restored between 1853 and 1884, the original church was built by well-known York Master Mason John Foreman between 1525 and 1536. The majority of glass dates from the building of the church, and is by Anglo-Flemish artists, who also built the windows of the south transept of the Minster, including the famous Rose Window. Good examples of glass from this period are extremely rare, and the windows in St Michael's are particularly fine examples.

*A Local Guy*
In this church Guy Fawkes was baptised on 15 April 1570. His father, Edward Fawkes, was a church lawyer. Guy went to St Peter's Free School, then in Gillygate, now in Clifton. In 1580 his mother remarried following his father's death: his new stepfather, Dionis Bainbridge, was a Roman Catholic living in Scotton, Yorkshire. In 1591 he came of age and quickly squandered all of his inheritance. In 1593 he enlisted in the army of the King of Spain, and served in the Spanish Netherlands, now Holland and Belgium.

*Gunpowder Plot*
In 1604 his old school fellows Christopher and John Wright roped him into Gunpowder Plot. He hired a cellar under St Stephen's chapel, then the meeting place of the House of Lords, to blow it up on the day of the State Opening of Parliament – 5 November 1605. Thus King, Lords, Bishops and Commons would all be destroyed and the King of Spain could invade from the Channel ports and there would be a Catholic uprising across the country.

*Fateful Letter*
But one of the conspirators, Tresham, warned his relative Lord Monteagle not to go to the State Opening. This letter was shown to James I, the cellars were searched and Guy Fawkes was caught with 32 hundredweight of gunpowder.

*Tortured For Three Months*
He was taken to the Tower and tortured for three months until eventually he revealed the names of his fellow conspirators. King James indicated in a letter that 'the gentler tortures are to be first used unto him, *et sic per gradus ad mia tenditur*, and so God speed your goode worke'. Torture was contrary to English common law, unless authorised by the King or Privy Council. Eventually, Guy Fawkes' spirit broke and he confessed that the plot was confined to five men. 'He told us that since he undertook this action he did every day pray to God he might

*St Michael-le-Belfry church – in this church Guy Fawkes was baptised on 15 April 1570.*

perform that which might be for the advancement of the Catholic faith and saving his own soul'. The following day he recounted the events of the conspiracy, without naming names, but later he named his fellow plotters, having heard that some of them had already been arrested.

*Spirit Broken*

His final signature, a barely legible scrawl, is testament to his suffering at the hands of his torturers. There is no direct evidence as to which horrendous methods of torture were used on Guy Fawkes, although it is almost certain that they included the manacles, hot irons, and probably also the rack. On Friday, 31 January 1606, he was taken with other conspirators to the Old Palace Yard at Westminster and hung, drawn and quartered, 'in the very place which they had planned to demolish in order to hammer home the message of their wickedness'. Following his death, there were bonfires and rejoicing throughout the country; a custom which remains in England to this day.

## *St Mary, Bishophill Junior*

The imposing church has watched over the streets of Bishophill for over a thousand years. In the area are there are several haunted sites, houses and churches. For generations the surrounding land and the buildings upon it were part of the life of the church.

*St Mary Bishophill Junior – in the area there are several haunted sites, including houses and churches.*

*Upside Down Roman Walls*

Despite its name, it is one of the oldest churches in York, and presumably the daughter church of the nearby St Mary Bishophill Senior, which possibly has Roman origins. The church was already around 100 years old when William the Conqueror landed. It is the only standing church tower not to have been burnt down by him in 1069, or rebuilt. The tower is entirely built of reused Roman stones from the nearby walls, but the top stones have been used as foundations for the church and the Roman foundations in the top – so it is the Roman walls upside down! Inside the great tower arch is what is thought to be a reused Roman arch, perhaps from some great public building, forum, or Roman predecessor of Micklegate Bar.

*Haunted Ballroom*

On the site of what was to become a famous dancing school, there once stood a building which was connected with the upkeep of the church. It sometimes seems that ghosts may outlast the buildings of their own time and continue to haunt the newer buildings constructed to replace them. The modern hall has inherited an intriguing supernatural recording. An invisible scene from centuries past slowly unfolds, as the stillness of the hall is broken.

*Money, Lovely Money!*

Somewhere back in time a figure is counting money, possibly, from an old church collection box. An invisible box of coins is emptied noisily onto an invisible table. The clatter of coins spilling out onto the table surface is followed by silence. Then, slowly and methodically each coin is heard to slide across the table surface, to fall rattling into a metal box, presumably resting in the lap of the ghostly counter. The click, click, click, of the coins into the box grows louder and louder. Until the last coin drops into the metal box, and its lid is slammed shut with a loud bang, and silence once again returns to the hall, until the invisible counter returns again to recount his coins.

## *St Savour's Parish*

*Final Nightmare*

One of the fears which haunted the imagination of writer Edgar Allan Poe was the terrifying prospect of being buried alive – the premature burial. Over the years many instances have been recorded of corpses apparently reviving, just as the lid was about to be firmly fixed down upon their coffin.

There are even more nightmarish accounts of bodies being discovered outside coffins when sealed vaults have been reopened in order to add further family members to the vault, their hands battered and torn, evidence of their frantic attempts to find some way out of their living tomb. There are accounts of floods and landslides in ancient graveyards where coffin lids have been dislodged and the insides of the lids are grooved by the torn nails of the occupant, as they tried to frantically escape their dark, silent prison, deep below the ground.

*Somewhere back in time a figure is counting money, possibly from an old church collection box.*

*St Savour's Parish – where the sexton reopened the sealed family vault and forced open the lid from the coffin.*

*Coffin lids have been unearthed, showing grooves made by the torn nails of the occupant, as they tried to frantically escape their dark, silent prison, deep below the ground.*

*The Rapacious Sexton*

An experience of this type has been connected with the churchyard of St Savour's Parish. Many years ago it was traditional to bury people with their personal jewels, and a sexton of the parish, aware that a number of valuable rings had been buried with a corpse, decided to steal them for himself.

Returning to the graveyard late at night when all the family mourners had left, he reopened the sealed family vault and forced open the lid from the coffin. By lamplight, he set about his gruesome task of cutting the rings from the body, but in doing so, he cut into the fingers of the apparent corpse.

His victim was not dead, but had been buried alive whilst in a coma, and the pain and flow of blood from her hands awakened her, so terrorising the rapacious sexton. To the horror of the sexton, but the delight of her family and friends, she was returned to her home.

Reports of the events reached the authorities, and the sexton's home was searched to reveal a large collection of jewellery; which it was believed had been over the years removed from less lively corpses. He was dismissed in disgrace from his position. No charges were ever brought.

*The Sexton Returns?*

Many years later, there were a number of reports of people passing by the graveyard late at night and seeing the phantom figure of a darkly dressed man, wearing a top hat, who appeared to be leaning down deep into a grave. On being discovered he would hurry away darting between the gravestones.

## *St Martin-cum-Gregory church*

This is the saddest and most under-used medieval church surviving in York today. No longer used for worship, it has had a number of abortive new uses, including a mother's union centre and a shelter for the homeless. It was used for jumble and book sales, but this is not now possible due to defective wiring.

*Bizarre Cult*

Though most of the structure dates from the fifteenth century, the eighteenth century brick tower has reused Roman stones in its base and one of these has been further reused as an Anglo-Saxon cross shaft with vine-scroll on it. In the nineteenth century excavations in the churchyard revealed the remains of a Roman temple of Mithras. A fine carving of the god is

*Bizarre stone carvings outside another St Martin's church in York – St Martin le Grand.*

now in the Yorkshire Museum. This cult involved bizarre initiation rites, such as being buried alive, passing through fire and being covered with bull's blood and was very popular with the Roman military. St Martin was a soldier-saint (he cut his military cloak in two to give half to a beggar) – perhaps the early Christian church was putting a church to a soldier-saint here to suppress a pagan temple once popular with soldiers.

*Peckitts Memorial*

On the north aisle there is a memorial window by the York glass painter William Peckitt to his two daughters who died before him. He was to become one of York's best-known glass artists, and was responsible for much of the Minster's eighteenth-century glass. The west window of the north aisle is all from Peckitt's workshop. The central panel depicts an urn, and was painted and installed by his wife Mary in memory of her husband following his death in 1795. Perhaps fittingly William Peckitt is buried in the chancel of the church which to this day displays such fine examples of his skills.

*Graveyard Market*

From early medieval times until 1828, St Martin's churchyard and the area of Micklegate close by was the location of a wholesale butter market for the whole of Northumbria. The market was held on every day of the week except Sunday, and York was noteworthy as the largest collection point for wholesale butter for the London butter market. At the height of its popularity, it was estimated that almost five million pounds of butter passed through the churchyard each year – the majority of which would have supplied the insatiable London market.

The original butter market was established in Micklegate in 1662 and in 1722 an Act of Parliament laid down that a free market for butter should be held here. A butter stand was built in the street in 1764. It was a place where butter was weighed, searched and sealed, before being dispatched, first by butter boats to Hull, then onwards in ships of the contract fleet to London. The local merchants were the middle men in this thriving trade and over the centuries they made their homes in the busy streets around the market stand where butter was traded for over 160 years until its demolition in 1828.

*Close by notice the modern replacement for the medieval stocks, with only five holes.*

## *Holy Trinity Priory (1089-1538) – Micklegate*

This is the oldest monastic site in York, as there was a 'Minster of Canons' here before the Norman Conquest. It was destroyed in a fire in York in 1069 in the harrying of the North.

In 1089 it was given to the Benedictine Abbey of St Martin of Tours (Marmoutier) and became a daughter house or Priory. Most of present church was rebuilt after the great fire in York in 1137 and dates from late twelfth century. It was dissolved by Henry VIII (1536-8), but it continued as a parish church after the Dissolution. In 1551, the tower fell in a gale and destroyed the choir and transepts. So the church is now only half the height, length and width of pre-Dissolution church. But it is the only monastic church in York still in use.

*Stocks Broken*

Close by notice the modern replacement for the medieval stocks, with only five holes. Used from Anglo-Saxon times until 1837, they were a popular means of punishing minor offences such as drunkenness, resisting a constable or drinking alcohol during church services. Although the concept of public punishment may now seem strange and possibly even barbaric, it was accepted as the norm until the nineteenth century. It is only in recent times that prison has been used as a form of punishment; these buildings were previously used only as places to hold offenders prior to their trial or punishment. Public humiliation was a major part of punishment in stocks and pillories, which were often sited in the most public thoroughfares, in market squares or village greens. Even in large cities those being punished would be well known to the people of their neighbourhood, thereby increasing their shame. Audience participation was always a key element. The helpless victim would usually be subjected to a barrage of mockery and abuse and pelted with any rotten fruit and vegetables, mud, excrement, dead rats, and even stones, as they remained firmly restrained in the stocks for a number of hours or in some cases days!

*Holy Trinity Priory (1089-1538) with stocks nearby. Used from Anglo-Saxon times until 1837, they were a popular means of punishing minor offences.*

*What do you do with a drunken sailor?*
Legend says that there was a one-legged sailor with a peg leg who used to live in the area. He spent most of his time in the local alehouses where he would play for hours on his old accordion. Many of the locals felt sorry for him and would buy him drinks, and so he lived his life in a permanently drunken state. At the time one of the punishments for drunkenness and brawling in the streets was imprisonment in the stocks. The legend tells that, so frequent were the sailor's spells of imprisonment in the local stocks, that when the time came for the old stocks to be replaced the local carpenter made a set of stocks with five holes: one hole for the one-legged sailor, and four holes to contain two normal people! Others claim that the truth is that the stocks were being broken up for firewood about 100 years ago and a vicar rescued them, but one end was lost.

*Early in the Morning*
There are stories in the area of people out in the streets early in the morning hearing the faint sound in the distance of an accordion, and as they walk closer to where they believe the sound may be coming from they hear the tap, tap, tap on the pavement of a peg leg, as the phantom moves hurriedly away into the darkness. Could it be the drunken sailor still staggering around the desolate streets, unaware that he need never today fear a spell in the old stocks? The worst he may have to look forward to today would be an ASBO or perhaps a community service order.

## *All Saints church – Pavement*

There has been a church on this site since well before the Norman Conquest, and this is one of eight York churches to be mentioned in the Domesday Book. All Saints has always been one of the city's wealthiest parishes, and thirty-nine of the former Lord Mayors of the city are claimed to be buried in the church or its grounds.

*Ancient Landmark*
The tall tower of this church has long been one of the most graceful features of the city's skyline. The present tower is a nineteenth-century replica of the fifteenth-century original structure. Floodlit against the dark night sky, this imposing York skyline monument is a continuing reminder of the original lantern tower's purpose. In centuries past, a light would traditionally be kept burning, high up the tower to guide travellers through the now vanished Forests of Galtres.

*All Saints church, Pavement – thirty-nine of the former Lord Mayors of the city are claimed to be buried in the church or its grounds.*

It is claimed that the forest was so thick until around 2,000 years ago, that a squirrel could make its way over fifteen miles from the village of Crayke to York's city wall, leaping from branch to branch, without its feet once touching the ground below.

*Doom at the Door*

A fearsome creature crafted in dark metal forms the door handle to the great wooden door of All Saints church. Known as a 'Doom', the knocker is believed to be twelfth-century, and is therefore the oldest part of the church. It depicts a beast swallowing a human being. In the past a person pursued by the authorities was granted sanctuary in the church by merely grasping the ring of the handle. Similar grotesque Dooms are to be found at Adel in West Yorkshire and St Gregory's church in Norwich. Through the sturdy stone archway which surrounds the door have passed many thousands of souls, both living and dead. Though much of the church has been altered or disappeared, it still has many interesting and beautiful carvings in its carvings, windows and ancient books.

*The Funeral Guest*

In centuries past, funerals at the church held a special significance, for they prompted the appearance of what was claimed to be York's most beautiful ghost. The figure was that of a woman, wearing a long white dress which some claimed could have been a wedding dress. Others remained convinced that the garment which she wore was a shroud; it was described as being made of a shimmering white material which flowed down to the ground, as she floated gracefully close to the church doorway.

Her hair was often described as being extremely long, but always neatly dressed, in an attractive cluster of curls, and many people commented on her beauty and her completely natural appearance, beautiful skin with a clear complexion, and cheeks glowing with health. There appears to be no legend or tradition connected with her appearance. The only constant in the reports of her appearance is her apparent urge to be present during funeral services. She would beckon the procession into the safety of the church and would then vanish, as quickly and mysteriously as she had arrived, leaving behind only an atmosphere of stillness and tranquillity.

*A fearsome creature crafted in dark metal forms the door handle to the great wooden door; it depicts a beast swallowing a human being.*

## *St Mary's – Castlegate*

In 1868, during restoration work carried out on this site, an inscribed stone recording the dedication of a minster on this site in 1016, shortly after Cnut came to power, was discovered by workmen. The church is also recorded in the Domesday Book. During the fifteenth century the building was extensively restored and rebuilt; since that time little has changed and it remains one of the least altered medieval churches in York.

Connected with this old church is the strange account of a reincarnation. It is claimed that under hypnosis certain subjects are able to recall past lives. A lady by the name of Jane Evans made such a claim when she apparently regressed to a time when she was a Jewess called Rebecca, who was tragically caught up in the anti-Semitic riots of 1190.

*Escape from the Frenzied Mob*

Under hypnosis 'Rebecca' gave detailed descriptions of medieval York, and the terrible events of the riots. We know that during the riots many of York's Jewish population sheltered in Clifford's Tower, only to be pursued by the frenzied mob. As she relived her terrible night, she went on to describe how, with her family, she had escaped from the tower and sought shelter in the crypt of nearby St Mary's church in Castlegate: she was able to describe the inside of the crypt in great detail.

*Slaughtered in the Crypt*

Within minutes the blood-crazed mob battered their way into the crypt, and 'Rebecca' described in lurid detail how she and her entire family were butchered by the mob. The whole horrifying tale was revealed in a shocking BBC television documentary called *The Bloxham Tapes*, a study of the work of an acknowledged expert in regression hypnosis therapy, Mr Arnall Bloxham of Bristol.

*Amazing Discovery*

Sceptics dismissed the account, as no crypt existed in St Mary's, and the whole account was almost forgotten. Some years later in 1975, a remarkable thing happened. Workmen at St Mary's discovered a small burial chamber, exactly matching the descriptions given by 'Rebecca' in her account of that horrible night. Could this be at last proof that reincarnation is possible? If not, how could it be that Jane Evans was able to describe in such detail a burial chamber which at the time no one even knew existed?

## *The church of the Holy Trinity – Micklegate*

Holy Trinity Priory was founded by St Oswald in the tenth century, and was later given by Ralph Paynel to the great French Monastery of Marmoutier around 1098. His gift also included substantial lands throughout England in Lincolnshire and Buckinghamshire.

### *Fateful Fire*

The Priory rose to significant power and wealth and also included in York: St Martin-cum-Gregory, All Saints on North Street and St Cuthbert's on Peasholme Green. The original monastery covered an area of some seven acres, as well as a sizeable portion of the medieval walled town. On 4 June 1137 a great fire swept though York. At the time the majority of buildings were constructed from tinder, wood, lathe and daub, and because of the overcrowding the fire spread quickly through the city destroying everything in its path. The present church dates from the rebuilding following the fire. Interestingly, towards the end of the Hundred Years' War, when all the French properties were seized by Act of Parliament, Holy Trinity Priory uniquely seems to have retained its independence; the end of the Priory came just over a century later with the Dissolution.

### *Series of Disasters*

One of the oldest ghost stories in the whole of York concerns the church of the Holy Trinity in Micklegate. Ever since the Revd S. Baring Gould, the writer of *Onward Christian Soldiers*, first collected the many eyewitness accounts in his book *Yorkshire Oddities*, this particular haunting has been included in ghostly guides to the North of England. Not too far from the church, possibly as long ago as medieval times, lived a small family.

The couple were young, and had just one baby child whom they adored. They lived happily and quietly until a series of mysterious disasters befell them. The father is believed to have died from injuries received in some long-forgotten accident. His grieving wife watched as he was interred in the church graveyard, taking what comfort she could from their one surviving infant child.

### *The Black Death*

Soon after, the child became ill, showing all the symptoms of the dreaded Black Death or plague. The worst plague in York's history was in 1604, when 3,512 people died – over one-third of the total population at that time. The mayor and council did all they could to deal with the plagues which ravaged the city in the seventeenth century, though some councillors fled the city and were fined for not doing their duty. The city's cats and dogs were all slain, which actually made things worse as the black rats which carried the disease were able to breed even faster.

The poor who contracted the plague were housed in camps, set up outside the city gates, at Hob Moor, and the Horse Fair on Gillygate, and it was probably to one of these that the grieving wife and her sick child were sent. Despite the mother's desperate care, the child soon died. In accordance with the regulations to prevent the spread of the dreaded disease, the infant's body was buried alongside other plague victims, in large pits outside the city walls. The loss proved too great for the young mother to bear, and she is said to have died shortly after from a broken heart.

Although husband and wife were united by burial in the same graveyard, the family remained separated even in death by the child's burial in unconsecrated ground, and they were never able to find eternal peace.

*Holy Trinity, Goodramgate. The first definite mention of the church is in the early twelfth century – some earlier documents which claim to mention the church in 1082 and 1093 are now believed to be forgeries.*

*Still Searching*
For many hundreds of years the ghost of the mother continued to appear, even in broad daylight, searching for her lost child. One version tells of how a mysterious female figure appears, carrying the infant, and returns it to the ghostly mother, before all three figures fade back into nothingness. Major building alterations were carried out to the church in 1886, and there does not appear to have been any visual evidence of the phantoms since 1890, and the church now seems quiet.

## *Holy Trinity – Goodramgate*

One of York's churches which may be easily overlooked, located off the roads of the city, and set in its own gardens in the angle of Petergate and Goodramgate.

*Forged Documents*
The first definite mention of the church is in the early twelfth century. Some earlier documents which claim to mention the church in 1082 and 1093 are now believed to be forgeries. The earliest parts of the present church date from the thirteenth century. With twelfth-century foundations and subsequent additions which span seven centuries, the history of the city is visible all around. Many past citizens of York are represented by the interesting collection of monuments and memorials. The late perpendicular east window contains fifteenth-century stained glass of exceptional quality and interest, and the seventeenth/eighteenth-century box pews are unique in the whole of York.

*Peeping through the Hagioscope*
Over on the south side of the church is a small private chapel, added to the main building during the fifteenth century. It was originally reserved for private worship by the de Howne family (who later became Holme), and was a bequest of Robert de Howne, who died in 1396. In this chapel private Mass was said for the family by a hired priest, whilst at the same time Mass was said for the rest of the congregation in the main body of the church. In order to allow the priest in the private chapel to observe the moments of consecration at the main altar, and thereby synchronise his ceremony in the de Howne chapel with that at the high altar, there is a small 'peep-hole' or 'squint' (properly referred to as a 'hagioscope') in the north-east corner of the chapel.

*Rumour has it that the headless body of the Earl may still occasionally be seen here, lurching between the tombstones in search of his missing head.*

*Man of Troubled Times*

Thomas Percy, the 7th Earl of Northumberland, was a man of action. He was born into times of political turmoil and religious strife, toward the second-half of the sixteenth century.

*Rebellion against the Queen*

His dissatisfaction with the rule of Queen Elizabeth and his desire for a religious Counter-Reformation, and his wish to see Mary Queen of Scots seize the royal throne, eventually led him to open rebellion. His fellow conspirator was the Earl of Westmorland. The pair led open rebellion in 1569 against the Protestant Queen Elizabeth, and called for the northern Catholics to rally to the cause. The ordinary people had little taste for the rebellion and after a brief campaign of battles and sieges in the North of England the rebellion crumbled.

The Earl of Westmorland fled to safety in France, whilst Thomas Percy, the Earl of Northumberland, fearing for his life, fled over the border to Scotland where he was subsequently captured. Despite the attempts of Philip II of Spain and Pope Pious V to ransom him, he was brought back to York in chains to be executed for the crime of High Treason.

*Off with his head!*

On 22 August 1572, the chosen day of execution, he stood before the assembled crowd defiantly at the scaffold which had been erected in Parliament Street. He declared that he would renounce neither his religion nor his deeds. As he went to his death he wore a precious relic given to him by Mary Queen of Scots – a thorn claimed to be from the crown of Christ, set in a cross of solid gold.

The executioner brought the axe down on the nobleman's neck, removing his head with one powerful blow. Though support for the rebellion had been scant, many people now looked upon him as a martyr. Those with a front-row seat next to the gallows pushed forward to soak their handkerchiefs in the blood pumping from the corpse of the now headless Earl. Many more scrambled to gather up the soaked and stained straw from the street around the execution site, as a gruesome souvenir of the day.

He was to become known to some as a Catholic martyr, 'Blessed Sir Thomas Percy'. Eventually as the crowds drifted away, his headless body was removed by two loyal servants for burial in the nearby church of St Crux.

*Ready, Heady, Cook*

The 'head of the traitor' was placed upon a pole in Micklegate Bar, where it gazed with sightless eyes to the street below. Traditionally heads would be placed on the Bar on either side of the central stone warrior on high spiked poles set in iron sockets. The authorities believed these gruesome warnings would endure for many years, and so, the heads were often parboiled to

Above left: *The 'head of the traitor' was placed upon a pole in Micklegate Bar, where it gazed with sightless eyes to the street below.*

Above right: *Throughout the city grotesque heads often peer down on unsuspecting visitors!*

preserve them and seasoned with cumin seed to deter the birds from picking at the flesh. Just a few years later in 1557 the economics of dealing with traitors were uncovered when it was agreed that the following item should be paid out of corporate funds with 'the expense of boiling, and carving, and setting up of carcasses of the late traitors, about the city, amounting to 12s – 6d'.

It has also been recorded that the original poles, on which the heads were set, lasted until the end of the nineteenth century, at which time a tenant of the Bar chambers chopped them up for firewood!

*No head for heights!*

For only two winters did the citizens of York gaze up to Micklegate Bar and the lifeless head of Sir Thomas Percy. In 1574 James Torr recorded in his book the event of 'the Earl of Northumberland's head stolen in the night from Micklegate Bar by persons unknown'. The probability is that the head was removed by some pious Catholic sympathiser. We know that following the execution even as the head was laying in the toll booth on Ouse Bridge awaiting boiling, a saddler by the name of William Testimond cut some of the hairs of the beard of the recently departed Earl of Northumberland and wrapped them in a paper on which he wrote, 'the hair of the beard of the good Earl of Northumberland'.

Later Testimond was brought before the High Commission to explain his words, and his precious relic was confiscated! Whoever the thief was we shall never know, but it is believed that the head was given a Christian burial in Holy Trinity, Goodramgate. Rumour has it that the headless body of the Earl may still occasionally be seen, lurching between the tombstones here in search of his missing head: a legend that gives chilling significance to Thomas Percy's last words before execution: 'I am a Percy, in life and in death.'

## *St Crux – Holy Cross*

This was the largest medieval parish church in York after its rebuilding in 1424. An Italianate brick tower said to have been designed by Sir Christopher Wren was added in 1697, and for many years the church was claimed to be one of York's finest places of worship. The church was closed around 1880 after becoming unsafe, and attempts to raise sufficient funds to rebuild it were unsuccessful. It was demolished in 1887, although some of the church's stonework was used to build the St Crux Parish Hall at the bottom of The Shambles.

*Chopped outside the church*

High-class executions often took place in the area known as Pavement close to the church. The chosen method of execution was by the axe. One nobleman to lose his head in such a fashion was the Earl of Northumberland, executed in 1572 for his part in the northern Catholic rebellion against Elizabeth I. His execution was carried out on a new scaffold specially set up for the purpose. His sword was first symbolically broken at the altar of St Crux church. His body was later buried by his servants in St Crux churchyard in an unmarked grave. Replicas of his helmet, sword and gauntlets were hung up in the church, but were transferred to All Saints Pavement, to which the parish church of St Crux was joined in 1885. Old stories in York tell of at least two ghosts who were associated with the church of St Crux.

*Musical Nightwatchmen!*

One of these stories tells of a female phantom who was a great music lover. She was described as a beautiful figure always dressed in white, who first appeared from the direction of the churchyard, and was always on hand to welcome the men from the 'York Waits' as they passed by the church. This ancient order takes its name from the ancient city band of York, the earliest evidence for which is to be found in fourteenth-century records. Before they turned to music full-time, the Waits had been a type of nightwatchmen, and although their guard duties diminished, they continued to keep the night watches in the weeks leading up to Michaelmas; playing at various points throughout the city to mark the hours and wake the citizens. In York as in many towns, they were employed by the Lord Mayor as the city's own band of musicians. They were paid and liveried by the Corporation to play on public occasions. The band is known to have been in continuous existence for at least five hundred years until its abolition in 1836.

*Some of the church's stonework was used to build the St Crux Parish Hall at the bottom of The Shambles.*

*Early Groupie?*
The female phantom joined the men from the Waits as they passed the church, following the group at a short distance, stopping whenever they did, listening intently to their playing, and then moving along with them, but always at a respectful distance behind. We are told that in the early days this unusual groupie alarmed some of the performers, but eventually her frequent appearances caused them to look for her and sometimes to call out to her, but always without reply. The men, clad in their splendid scarlet livery and followed by the lady in white, always followed the same route, along Colliergate they went, into King's Square, and then, just as they turned into Goodramgate, she disappeared as suddenly as she had arrived.

*Early man – at the Window*
The second story associated with the church is of a tall, bold-looking man, who was often seen standing by one of the windows, looking out intently into the street. What was unusual about the ghost is that he always appeared in the very early hours of the morning. He was to become a familiar sight to many of the women of York going to their cleaning jobs, long before the rest of the city was awake. The women often called out to him, but he was said never to appear outside the church, and understandably at this stillest hour of the morning, none of the women were ever tempted to venture inside the building to investigate further, as they hurried by to work.

## *St Johns – Micklegate*

*Bodies Below the Pavement*
To the south side of the river Ouse lies the parish of St John's, Micklegate. Back in the nineteenth century it was the second most crowded parish in the whole of York, with over a thousand residents crammed into less than two acres. Its small graveyard to the south side of the church had been reused so many times that the vestry made a resolution in 1845 to close it, however a number of vaults were still available within the church, although nine years later the incumbent stated that he had no intention of using them. By 1966 increasing traffic in Micklegate demanded a road-widening scheme and the former parishioners' graves are now covered forever by the pavement outside the church. The building was closed in 1934, and its fittings dispersed in 1938 when it was taken over by the Corporation.

*Nathaniel's Painful Distemper*
Only one ledger stone remains in the old church. This marks the burial place of Nathaniel Wilson, who was also commemorated by a wall monument which sets out his many virtues:

> An East Country Merchant; unblameable in his dealings and commerce. He was an affectionate, loving husband; a kind indulgent father; a good master, a sincere friend; a charitable, devout Christian; and a zealous advocate for the constitution, in Church and State. After he had been afflicted many years with a painful distemper, which he bore with great patience and resignation he departed this life the 9th Day of December 1726 in the seventy-first year of his age.

Whatever Nathaniel's 'painful distemper' may have been, it still seems to disturb his rest 280 years later. The sinister footfalls which sometimes echo along the upstairs passageway in the church, and the heavy echoing that reverberates on the old stone staircase which leads towards it, are claimed to be those of his resident ghost.

# Chapter 5
# Gravestones

*One Giant Graveyard*

The city of York, over 2,000 years old, is in reality one giant graveyard. Wherever and whenever archaeologists or workmen sink a spade into the ground, more often than not, the bones of its previous occupants are discovered, surrounded by their homes and possessions. Roman laws forbade burial within the city walls, and their cemeteries are to be found alongside the approach roads into the city. To date, fifteen cemeteries and many individual graves have been discovered, mainly in the suburbs, beneath the buildings of later centuries. During excavations made in Coppergate between 1976 and 1981 the Viking city of Jorvik was discovered; it included a collection of late ninth-century bones. Following the Norman conquest, the Minster which was built on the site of the original Roman fortress was consumed by a terrible fire which swept through the city destroying many buildings and parish churches, but by the early twelfth century, York had recovered its prosperity, and by the early thirteenth century the Minster was rebuilt, rising like a phoenix from the ashes. The expanding city contained some forty-five parish churches, a nunnery, four monasteries, a number of religious almshouses or hospitals, most of them with their own graveyard.

*1,000 Medieval Corpses Exhumed*

The city also had a growing Jewish community who bought land from John le Romeyn, the sub-dean of the Minster, on which to establish a Jewish cemetery, at a place which became known appropriately as Jewbury. Prior to this, the laws of the land dictated that all Jews had to be taken to London for burial. The site was in use until 1290 when by order of Edward I, all Jews were expelled from England, the remains of the medieval Jews lay undisturbed here until the site was excavated in 1982 in advance of the creation of a supermarket car park. The remains of almost 1,000 individuals were excavated and examined scientifically. In 1984 the Chief Rabbi, Lord Jakobovits, put a stop to the examination of the bones, and they were re-interred by a plaque in a raised flower bed. Later, the decision was made to remove them to a Jewish cemetery in Manchester. The scientific examination of the graveyard was the only large-scale excavated Jewish burial ground in Europe and revealed a number of important findings. It found that the skeletons were aligned north to south, some disarticulated, perhaps brought a distance for burial, some of the coffins were very substantial – another indication that the corpses may have travelled for some distance. There was very little disturbance of previous burials, which indicated an orderly cemetery. Although no markers were discovered, it is possible that these were wooden. The average height was 5ft 5in for a male 5ft 1in for a female which is believed to have been slightly shorter than the rest of the Christian population of York at the time. It also seems that burials were clustered by sex and age, with women living slightly longer. The most common causes of death appeared to be Anaemia and Tuberculosis.

*Grave Concerns about the Drinking Water*

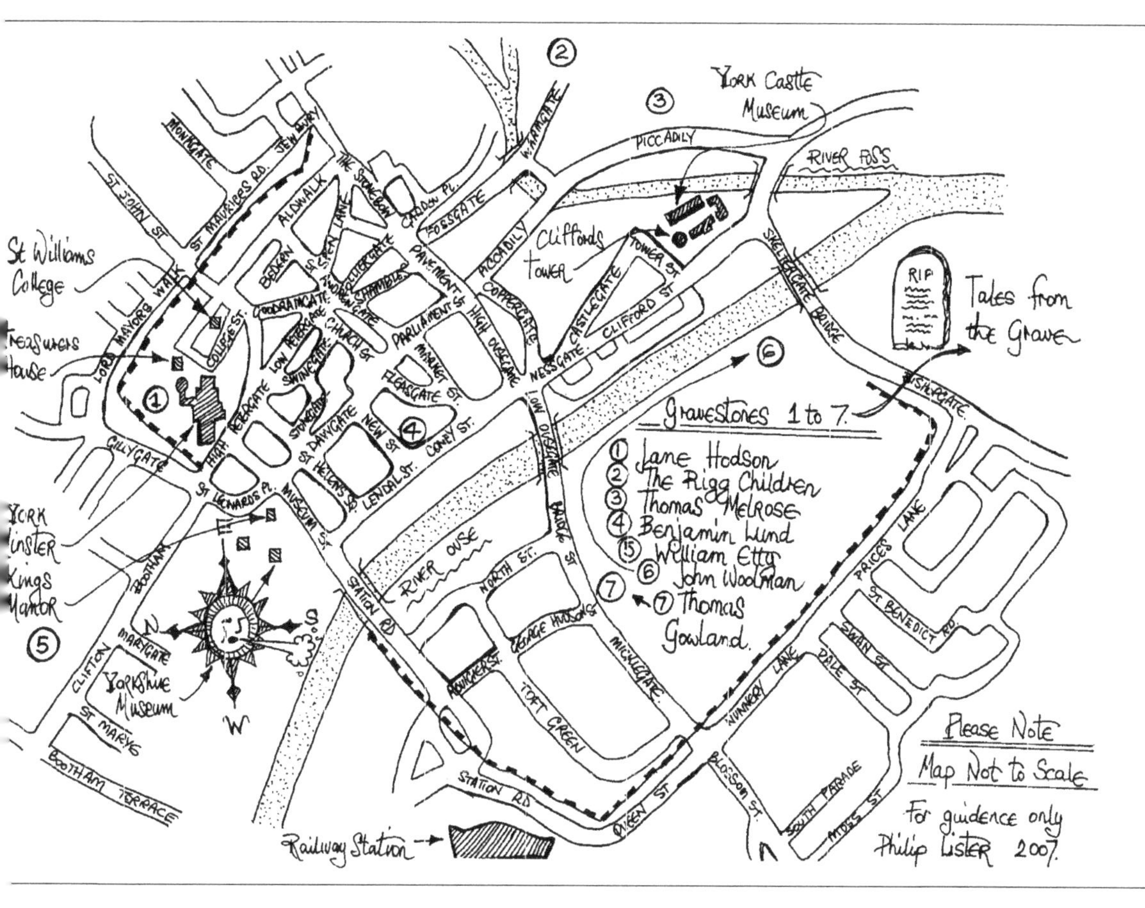


*A map of the city showing the location of the graves of Jane Hodson, the Rigg children, Thomas Melrose, Benjamin Lund, William Etty, John Woolman and Thomas Gowland.*

By the late thirteenth century some of the smaller churches had closed; later, under Henry VII, the monasteries were dissolved, and the buildings were plundered of their stone by the local population. Three hundred years later, in the sixteenth century, in an anti-religious climate, York Corporation obtained an Act of Parliament to reduce the number of parish churches from forty to twenty-five. Most of the redundant churches were sold, the buildings then demolished, and their graveyards disappeared under new buildings. By the nineteenth century the population of York was rising dramatically, and the remaining graveyards were inadequate to cope with the rising tide of corpses requiring burial. Graves had originally been dug to a depth of around two meters, but the ground had risen due to the sheer volume of bodies, and in many cases the graves had risen two meters above the ground. The graves were often too shallow, so the authorities heaped more earth onto the graveyards to cover the burials, which made the ground rise even faster. Very few houses had piped water supplies and were dependent for drinking water on wells in their yards and cellars. Unfortunately many of these were in close proximity to the many graveyards spread throughout the city. Two of the biggest killers during the nineteenth century were cholera and typhoid – both waterborne diseases. Great numbers of infected corpses were buried in the city's graveyards and the rainwater which fell on the graveyards would seep through the coffins and corpses and into the hundreds of wells throughout the city, passing the disease on to the next generation. A terrible cycle of death was set up from house to graveyard and back again.

*The Resurrection Men Await*

Another problem of the shallow graves was that the freshly buried corpses were very vulnerable to body snatchers or 'Resurrection Men' as they became known. Before the Anatomy Act of 1832, it was not possible to obtain corpses legally for medical dissection, apart from the occasional hanged felon from York's Knavesmire gallows. On some occasions, when the condemned man had been hanged he would be cut down and paraded through the streets for the further amusement of the bawdy crowd. Medical men – knives and saws at the ready – would often attend public hangings, waiting for the time when the crowd became bored with events, and they could seize the corpse. It was permitted by law for them to butcher the recently executed on their dissection tables for the purpose of anatomical research – hardly a pleasant thought for the condemned man or his family as they made their way to the Knavesmire on execution day! The supply of hanged felons was never enough to supply the ever-growing demand for fresh corpses, so they were often stolen from the graveyards – a good reason why the rich paid more to be buried inside the churches, where they were much more likely to be safe from the body snatchers. York was ideally placed for the illegal body trade, being located halfway between the emerging medical centres of Edinburgh and London, and with an excellent daily stagecoach service: on some trips the coach driver may have had more dead passengers than live ones.

*Sadly the cemetery became a derelict overgrown wilderness.*

*Revolting Scenes in the Churchyards*

In 1836 Thomas Hodgson and W.S. Campion, two York solicitors, published a prospectus proposing the flotation of the York General Cemetery Co. Its opening statement was so forthright that they found it necessary to stress that it was not an exaggeration.

> In few places in the kingdom are the above evils (those which attend burial places) so conspicuous as in the city of York, with its burial places in the central and most populous parts of the city – confined in space – surrounded with buildings – and crowded with dead. The inhabitants of houses adjoining most of the churchyards can bear testimony to the revolting scenes that continually occur in them, where scarcely a grave is made to receive the body of one person without disturbing that of another, and exposing the remains of departed relatives and friends in a manner offensive to the senses – shocking to the feelings – and prejudicial to the health of the inhabitants.

The two solicitors failed to generate sufficient support but by 1837 the York Cemetery Co. had opened its graveyard outside the city, 'where all citizens regardless of creed or rank could be buried undisturbed'. Still, many citizens were reluctant to use it as they had traditionally buried their families in the historic city graveyards, and they wished to be buried close to their relatives; and even some of the city clergy resisted the new cemetery, seeing it as an attack on their income generated by the burials in the church graveyard, no matter how gruesome those burials may have proved to be.

*A Funeral to Remember*

In the 1840s, journalist Hargrove of the *York Herald* led a press campaign to have the old city graveyards closed. He recorded incidents of children seen playing in Walmgate with a human skeleton which was still articulated, and a dog seen running down Coney Street with a part-eaten human leg in its mouth. He also recalled the ordeal of one bitter winter's day, attending a funeral at St Sampson's churchyard, which was waterlogged. He described the family of the deceased along with the mourners sliding off the duck boards placed beside the open grave, ankle-deep in the mud and sludge, and the coffin, after having being lowered down into the grave, needing large stones placed on top, to prevent it floating back up to the surface in the freshly dug, waterlogged grave, filled with a putrid black pool of foul, stinking, greasy liquid.

Following the 1852/3 Public Health Acts, all burials inside churches and within urban graveyards were forbidden, and by 1855 the York Board of Health had closed the remaining city-centre graveyards. Since those times, two further new cemeteries have been opened in York, by religious communities. In addition to these and the Quaker burial ground, the only cemetery in current use is the public cemetery, which now covers a 24-acre site. Sadly the original company went into voluntary liquidation in 1966, but the cemetery and its buildings were bought in 1987 by the York Cemetery Trust, who run it as an active graveyard and as an excellent educational and ecological resource.

Earlier in my journey through this most fascinating and historic city I have visited many of the legends and myths and ghosts and phantoms which make it famous throughout the world. In my concluding chapter I would like to take you on a tour of just a few of the gravestones of some of the equally fascinating citizens who lived before, for I believe that every gravestone is like a page from a history book, a snapshot of a life in time. The difference is that these pages and this history book are carved from stone.

*The city of York, over 2,000 years old, is in reality one giant graveyard.*

## *Jane Hodson*

## *York Minster*

Buried in the south choir aisle of the Minster is the wife of Dr Phineas Hodson, who was a former Chancellor of York. The name of the lady is Jane Hodson, and a monument in Latin placed on the wall nearby tells us more about her life.

*Like a Virgin*

She died in labour on the 2 September 1636, aged thirty-eight years, and she was buried in the south choir on the same day, which leads me to think that the event of her death was not entirely unexpected.

> She was the best of wives, who, having blest her husband with numerous progeny of both sexes, at last in her twenty-fourth labour – she fell like a sentinel on duty with the most perfect steadiness and tranquillity of mind, in so early a period of life and such unfaded bloom of beauty she had the appearance of a virgin rather than the mother of so many children.

It seems hard to believe that a woman of only thirty-eight years could produce twenty-four children – if she conceived each child immediately after the birth of the previous one she would have been constantly pregnant for an unbroken period of eighteen years! What is more likely is that a large number of Jane's pregnancies never reached full term, and she lost a number of premature babies; this is also borne out by the fact that records can only be found for the baptism of fourteen children from the marriage. The earliest record of baptism is in 1615, at which time Jane was just seventeen years of age. If the inscription is to be believed she devoted the whole of her adult life to producing children.

## *The Rigg Children's Monument*

## *St Lawrence's, Lawrence Street*

Life in Victorian York was tough. It was common for people to have large families, and sadly also common that many of their children would not survive beyond their first few years of life. In some areas of the city, infant mortality could be as high as 40 per cent; a harsh fact of the times, which is borne out by countless epitaphs to children on Victorian gravestones.

*Early Heartbreak*

No doubt, every parent whilst never forgetting the pain of losing so many of their children at such a tender age, also felt the pride and relief as their surviving children grew towards adulthood. All the more difficult to comprehend the pain which must have been suffered by John and Ann Rigg, the son and daughter-in-law of Thomas Rigg, a local nurseryman and seedsman. The couple worked hard in the family business, and Ann also produced some fourteen children. Sadly, six of them succumbed to the many childhood ailments which were common at the time.

*Death in the Afternoon*

By 1830 some of her surviving eight children were approaching adulthood and the sadness of their earlier bereavements may have eased a little, when on the fateful summer's afternoon of the 19 August a horrible tragedy struck.

Six of her children perished in a tragic boating accident on the river Ouse when the rowing boat they were in was run down by another larger boat. Below a draped urn a decaying monument lists their names, followed by a verse specially composed by the Victorian hymn-writer, James Montgomery.

Ann Guthrie Rigg – aged 19
Thomas Gorwood Rigg – aged 17
Eliza Rigg – aged 16
John Rigg – aged 15
James Smith Rigg – aged 7
Charles Rigg – aged 6

Mark the brief story of a summer's day!
At noon, Youth, Health
and Beauty launched away;
Ere eve, Death couch'd the bark,
and quenched their light;
Their parents' home was desolate at night;
Each pass's alone, that gulf no eye can see;
They met next moment in Eternity.
Friend, Kinsman, Stranger,
dost thou ask me where?
Seek God's right hand
and hope to find them there.

Horrified parents throughout the city heard of the heartbreaking events of the afternoon of 19 August, and newspapers throughout the country carried graphic reports of the drowning of the Rigg children.

Six years later when their broken-hearted grandfather Thomas Rigg died aged eighty-nine years, he directed in his will that his property should be sold to educate the only two grandchildren who had survived from this large family, his two remaining granddaughters.

## *Thomas Melrose*

## *Former site of St George's graveyard – George Street*

Here in the public garden situated in the location of the former graveyard of St George's church are to be found a number of markers commemorating members of the Melrose family. It is believed the first member of the family to settle in York during the mid-eighteenth century was Walter Melrose, a farmer's son, who travelled from his home in Peeblesshire. He set up a family business as fellmongers (a smelly and unpleasant business preparing animal skins for the tanners) which was to endure in York for five generations, in what became known as 'Melrose Yard' in the Warmgate area of the city. The above gravestone is for Thomas Melrose who was a nephew of the youngest of Walter's sons, James. We believe that for a number of years Thomas worked as a skinner in London, but by the time of his death he had returned to his family here in York.

*Tough Part of the City*

Warmgate had the reputation of a rough, tough area, notorious for housing the large numbers of Irish immigrants who fled to England following the potato famine in their home country. For many years during the nineteenth century the area had a reputation for violence, crime, prostitution and drunkenness. None of this seemed to effect the Melrose family, and founder Walter was eventually joined by three of his sons as the business became established.

*Bride Whose Father Owned a Brewery!*

The youngest of these was James Melrose, and his grandson, also named James, was the centenarian who married Elizabeth Stephenson, the daughter of a Beverly brewer. His father-in-law gave him a job in the family brewery, and after learning his new trade eventually James returned to York, where he entered into partnership with John Roper the owner of a local brewery. The partnership worked well and the business prospered, until eventually in 1875 the unmarried John Roper died leaving the brewery and his house in Clifton to his partner.

*Amazing Achievement*

The freedom afforded by this legacy offered James Melrose the opportunity to expand his business and public service interests; after handing over the running of his brewery business to his eldest son he became Chairman of York Racecourse Committee, and Treasurer of York County Hospital. He held directorships in a number of York companies and served as Lord Mayor of the city in 1876. A greatly respected member of the community, he died in 1928 in his 101st year – an amazing achievement for the great-grandson of the humble, hard-working Walter Melrose who had struggled to establish his business in one of the toughest areas of the city just 180 years earlier.

## *Benjamin Lund*

## *St Martin-le-Grand, Coney Street*

*The Empty Grave*

One of only a handful of gravestones which remain outside the church marks the passing of Benjamin Lund. What may appear strange is the fact that he was actually buried in a vault under the vestry of the church itself, so that the gravestone marks an empty grave. He was a former parish clerk who bought his freedom as a printer in 1755, and some eight years later succeeded the previous clerk, Richard Jackson, who had served in the post for an amazing forty-eight years.

*Still trying to beat the record?*

Benjamin became a loyal servant to the church, and his name frequently appears on the parish registers as one of the required witnesses at marriage services. However if his ambition was to beat his predecessor's amazing record of service as parish clerk he was to be disappointed – he failed by just one year! It may be a strange thought but it is almost as if by being buried beneath the very vestry in which during his lifetime he must have carried out many of his parochial duties, Benjamin is still on duty, still trying in some strange way to better his predecessor's record of service.

## *William Etty*

## *St Olave's, Marygate*

*Started Work Early*

A large chest tomb marks the grave of possibly York's most famous artist, William Etty (1787-1849). One of the ten sons of a miller and gingerbread maker, at just twelve years of age he became an apprentice in a printing works in Hull, where he remained for the next seven years. Aged nineteen, with financial help from his uncle he left to become a student of art at the Royal Academy Schools in London. However, his submissions of works to the Academy Exhibitions were consistently rejected and for a number of years his work was ignored.

*Overnight Success after Eighteen Years*

In his mid-thirties he travelled in Italy, and inspired, he painted his first major work, 'Pandora Crowned by the Seasons', which was exhibited at the Royal Academy; it was so well received that it was purchased by his old tutor Sir Thomas Lawrence. After eighteen years of study and struggle William had become an overnight success; the Academy awarded him an ARA, and he went on to show 136 paintings in total, and build a reputation as a great artist.

He is remarkable for being the only major British painter before the twentieth century to have specialised in depictions of the nude, often in the face of public censure. His subjects included figures from classical myth, history and the Bible. Although he spent a great deal of his adult life in London, he retained contact with the city of his birth, and on one occasion was so concerned to hear that the Corporation was demolishing the barbicans and posterns of the city walls, he wrote in support to those opposed to further destruction: 'beware how you destroy your antiquities, guard them with religious care! They are what give you a decided character and superiority over other provincial cities. You have lost much, take care of what remains'.

*The Final Exhibition*
Eventually he retired from life in London in 1848, and returned to York, the city of his birth. One wish alone remained for him now to gratify; he desired to see a 'gathering' of his pictures. With great difficulty and exertion he was enabled to assemble the great majority of them from various parts of the British Isles. So numerous were they that the walls of the large hall he hired in London for their exhibition were almost completely covered. This finally took place during the summer of 1849. On 13 November of the same year he died. He received the honours of a public funeral in his native city of York, and was later to be commemorated by a statue paid for by public subscription and carved by George Walker Milburn. It stands outside the City Art Gallery which today houses many of Etty's works.

## *John Woolman*

### *Friends' Burial Ground, Bishophill*

*The Long Journey from New York to Old York*
In September 1772, John Woolman, an itinerant Quaker preacher from Mount Holly, New Jersey, New York arrived in the city having walked all the way from Westmorland. A highly principled Quaker, he refused to travel by stagecoach. He wrote in his diary:

> Stagecoaches frequently go upwards of one hundred miles in twenty-four hours; and I have heard Friends say in several places that it is common for horses to be killed with hard driving, and that many others are driven till they grow blind. Post-boys pursue their business, each one to his stage, all night through the winter. Some boys who ride long stages suffer greatly in winter nights, and at several places I have heard of their being frozen to death. So great is the hurry in the spirit of this world, that in aiming to do business quickly and to gain wealth the creation at this day doth loudly groan. As my journey hath been without a horse, I have had several offers of being assisted on my way in these stagecoaches, but have not been in them; nor have I had freedom to send letters by these posts in the present way of riding, the stages being so fixed, and one boy dependent on another as to time, and going at great speed, that in long cold winter nights the poor boys suffer much.

*The End of a Great Campaigner*
For the previous twenty-five years Woolman had travelled in America, preaching on many topics, including slavery. Working on a non-confrontational, personal level, he individually convinced many Quaker slave-holders to free their slaves. Early in 1772 he set passage to England to expand his ministry, speaking to Quakers at the London yearly meeting. The Friends there were persuaded to oppose slavery in their Epistle (a letter sent to other Friends in other places), and he continued his journey through northern England; in September of the same year he arrived in York, weakened and weary from his travels. It was originally planned that he would stay with William Tuke and his family in Castlegate, but, repulsed by the foul, noisy, stinking streets of the city centre, he asked if it would be possible to stay in a quieter place, in order to rest and regain his failing health. Alternative accommodation was offered by Thomas and Sarah Priestman in Almery Garth in Marygate, away from the city walls, but within days his condition worsened and he became seriously ill with the dreaded smallpox, and within one month he died.

*A highly principled Quaker, John Woolman refused to travel by stagecoach, many of which were based at the Olde Starre Inn.*

*Simple Burial*

Quaker beliefs deplored 'the vain and empty custom of erecting monuments over the bodies of dead Friends by stones, inscriptions, tombstones, etc', and most burials were very simple affairs eschewing any attempt to 'exalt the creature'. Despite this, here in the Friends' Burial Ground stands a monument with the inscription, 'near this stone rest the remains of John Woolman'.

Following his last directions, John Woolman was 'buried in an ash coffin made plain without any manner of superfluity; the corpse to be wrapped in cheap flannel, the expense of which I leave my wearing clothes to defray, as also the digging of my grave'.

I fully understand John's simple motives – but I cannot believe that the queue was too long when the sale of his 'wearing clothes' took place – bearing in mind that he died from the dreaded smallpox!

*His Spirit Lives On*

Although their acquaintance with the American preacher was brief, William Tuke and Thomas Priestman recognised the truth of his words, and soon the York Quakers vigorously supported the movement to abolish slavery; they supported the successful return of William Wilberforce in 1806 as MP for Yorkshire.

Back in his hometown of Mount Holly, New Jersey, a Memorial House was built between 1771 and 1783, which is on the site of John Woolman's orchard, the purpose of the association there being 'to keep alive the spirit and memory of John Woolman and seek those in whose lives that spirit may grow and serve', and each year in October a lecture is presented in his memory.

## *Thomas Gowland*

## *St Mary, Bishophill Senior*

The idea of building a railway between York and Leeds was first discussed in 1833. George Hudson, the chairman of the North Midland Railway was the line's main supporter. Hudson had already commissioned George Stephenson to build a line between Leeds and Derby. He now asked him to construct a railway between York and Leeds, and the company was commissioned to do so in 1836. Opened in 1839, the York & North Midland Railway became part of the great trunk route from London to York via Rugby and Derby. At £6,000 a mile, it was one of the cheapest railway lines ever to be built in Britain. The line was 72 miles long and contained 7 tunnels and 200 bridges.

*Hudson Scandal*
As a result of being involved in dubious business activities, George Hudson was forced to resign as chairman of the York & North Midland Railway in 1849. Six years later the company was taken over and became part of the North Eastern Railway. On 3 October 1851 an accident on the line was to take the life of Thomas Gowland, a goods train guard who worked on the railway. According to reports from the time, a heavily-laden coke train on which he was travelling had stopped at a signal at a place known as Burton Station Junction. Gowland was at this time on duty in the guards' van behind which was attached a single carriage. A following slowly moving train ran into the rear of the carriage, and as the buffers on the carriage were higher than those on the guards' van they crashed through it crushing Gowland, who died of his injuries two hours later. It transpired at the inquest which followed that it was normal practice at the time for following trains to run up behind the heavier coke trains in order to give them assistance in restarting from the signals, and it was stated that in three cases out of four the carriage at rear of the coke train would have come off worst in a collision, protecting the guard from any harm, (which, if my calculations are correct, meant he still had a 25 per cent chance of being killed in the event of a collision!) However, a verdict of accidental death was recorded.

## *Charlotte Hall*

## *York Public Cemetery*

Daughter of Thomas Fishburn Hall, a leather dresser and glove manufacturer of Clarence Street, Charlotte, who died at twenty-five years of age on 17 January 1837, was the first person to be buried in the graveyard here. Her tombstone records:

A lovely flower
removed, alas how soon
from the tender watchful care
that had reared and cherished it
to be the first transplanted
into this garden of death
yet not to continue here for every
but at the appointed season to be taken
into the paradise of God.
The first of many

At its peak over a thousand burials a year took place here, but by 1965 the number had fallen to 268, and the following year the York Cemetery Co. was wound up. York's rapidly increasing population at the beginning of the Industrial Revolution had caused increasing pressure on burial places in the city's churchyards, and in response to the ever-increasing demand for grave plots many municipal and privately owned cemeteries were established. York Cemetery was opened in 1837 and at the time was one of the first to be operated by a private company. For over one hundred years the cemetery expanded and prospered.

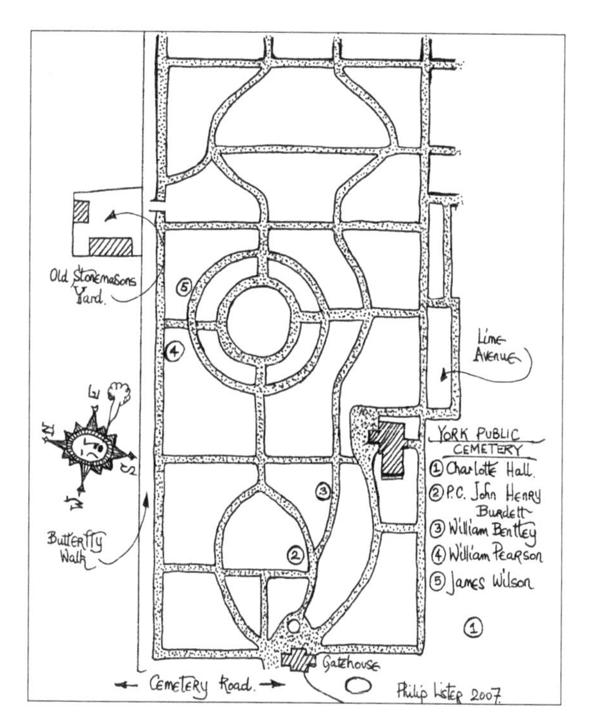


*A map of the cemetery showing the burial places of Charlotte Hall, PC John Henry Burdett, William Bentley, William Pearson and James Wilson in York Public Cemetery, Cemetery Road, York. Sadly the cemetery became a derelict overgrown wilderness, and in 1984 the roof of the chapel collapsed.*

*Abandoned to the Brambles*

However as the fashion for cremation advanced, inevitably the profits from burials dwindled and it became obvious that the cemetery could no longer be financially viable. Provision for this had been made over the years through the purchase of several stonemasons' businesses which subsidised the running of the site. In spite of this, in June 1966 the liquidators were called in to wind up the affairs of the company. Over the next thirteen years every saleable asset was stripped from the company. York City Council declined to become involved, and the site devolved to the Crown. The gates were locked, and over 120,000 bodies and two listed buildings were abandoned. Sadly the cemetery became a derelict overgrown wilderness, and in 1984 the roof of the chapel collapsed.

*A New Beginning*

A group of local people became involved and after almost three years of negotiation, York Cemetery was sold to them by the Crown Commission for a nominal sum. Now once again the cemetery has a number of grave plots available for sale, and the York Cemetery Education Service operates as part of the York Cemetery Trust, providing trails, tours and activities throughout the year. Additionally a comprehensive archive of almost 123,000 burial records is now available.

## *PC John Henry Burdett*

### *York Public Cemetery*

*Local Hero*

The recipient of a civic funeral in November 1905 following his death at just forty-eight years of age, from the complications following his tragic accident whilst attending a fire during the February of the same year. The funeral began with a parade from his home in Lowther Street to the cemetery, headed by the City Prize Band, and included the City, Rowntrees and the North Eastern Railway fire brigades. The entire police force of the city was present with the exception of the half-dozen officers who were required to control the huge crowds who turned out to pay their last respects to this gallant fire fighter.

*Dual Purpose Police Force*

In 1940 following the Fire Brigades Act of 1938, a professional fire brigade was formed in York. Prior to this for sixty-five years, the responsibility for fighting fires had fallen to the police. During this period half the beats in the city were designated as 'fire beats', and when the fire alarm was sounded, the policemen on fire beats would go to the 'fire house' to man the engines which attended the fire, whilst the others remained on duty and looked after the beat of their neighbouring colleague until the emergency was over.

*Fell Down The Coal Hole*

PC Burdett was on duty on 5 February 1905 when he saw flames at the railway station. Ss his beat on North Street was a fire beat he rushed to the scene and joined the rest of his colleagues in the goods yard. In the ensuing confusion he was passing a hose pipe over the wall of Cinder Lane when in the darkness he fell through a coal drop and broke his back. His accident paralysed him from the waist down and he was never to walk again: he was pensioned from the force in July, and died on the 31 October from blood poisoning from a massive bed sore.

Above left: *The entire police force of the city was present with the exception of the half-dozen officers who were required to control the huge crowds who turned out to pay their last respects to this gallant fire fighter.*

Above right: *During the thick of the fighting Sergeant Bentley was attacked from behind by three Cossacks and wounded in the neck.*

## *William Bentley*

## *York Public Cemetery*

*Into the Valley of Death Rode the Six Hundred*

A sergeant in the 11th Hussars based in Beverly, William Bentley had a long military career. He served with his regiment in the Crimea, and was to ride in the Charge of the Light Brigade on 25 October 1854. Out of the 110 cavalrymen of the 11th Hussars who rode into battle on that fateful day only twenty-five survived. The incident was later to be immortalised by Alfred Lord Tennyson's poem:

Cannon to right of them,
Cannon to left of them,
Cannon in front of them
Volley'd & thunder'd;
Storm'd at with shot and shell,
Boldly they rode and well,
Into the jaws of Death,
Into the mouth of Hell
Rode the six hundred.

*Into the Mouth of Hell*

During the thick of the fighting Sergeant Bentley was attacked from behind by three Cossacks and wounded in the neck. A young Canadian officer from his regiment, Lieutenant Alexander Roberts Dunn came to his rescue, and seeing his predicament galloped through a maze of the dead and dying and riderless horses to rescue him. Dunn parried and thrust at the assailants felling them all in a matter of minutes, but the wounded Bentley was still in dire straights – he was desperately hanging onto his horse by one of his stirrups, so Dunn dismounted, lifted his wounded colleague back into his own saddle, then belted the horse on the rump to send it galloping toward the British lines whilst making his own escape on foot.

*Swashbuckling Hero*

For his amazing bravery he was destined to be the first Canadian to be awarded the Victoria Cross, the British Empire's highest military honour for valour. Ironically born in 1833 at York (later named Toronto), Dunn, 6ft 3in tall, high in the saddle, blond-headed and handsome with a drooping moustache not only cut a glamorous romantic figure, he proved to be an outstanding cavalry officer. Altogether eleven Victoria Crosses were awarded during the Crimean War, but Dunn was the only officer in the Charge of the Light Brigade to receive the medal, and the only cavalry officer in the entire campaign to whom it was awarded. (In addition he was awarded the Crimean Medal with four clasps as well as the Turkish Medal).

*Life of Service*

Following the Crimean War, Bentley became a drill instructor with the Royal Wiltshire Regiment, eventually retiring to York after completing thirty-seven years of military service. He died seven years later, and was buried here with full military honours.

## *William Pearson*

## *York Public Cemetery*

*Take the Third Horse Home*

Some eighteen years after attending the funeral of his fellow survivor of the terrible Charge of the Light Brigade, William Bentley, another old soldier was to join him here in this garden of death. A member of the 17th Lancers, William Pearson had served in the Crimea under Sir George Orby Wombwell, who at the time of the Charge was just twenty-two years of age. Wombwell had joined the 17th Lancers two years earlier and was appointed ADC to Lord Cardigan for the campaign. When Wombwell reached the guns, his horse was killed under him; he mounted another, which was wounded, and he was shortly pulled off and taken prisoner. His sword and pistols were taken from him by some Russian Lancers; he managed to escape, catch another horse and ride hell for leather back to the British lines, hotly pursued by the Russians. Of the 147 of the 17th Lancers who rode into battle on 25 October 1854 for the Charge of the Light Brigade, only thirty-eight answered the roll call the following day.

*Horrors at the Hospital*

Poor William Pearson fared little better, and during the Charge he sustained a lance wound to his side and was sent to recuperate in Scutari Hospital, where he was tended by no less than Florence Nightingale. If the fate encountered by our soldiers in the field was swift and bloody

*On the day he was laid to rest here in his eighty-fourth year, a firing party was provided by the 5th Royal Irish Lancers.*

and violent, nothing could have prepared them for the horrors that awaited them here. A report in *The Times* by Thomas Chenery published on 14 October 1854 painted a graphic picture of the suffering so many were to endure:

> Not only are the men kept, in some cases for a week without the hand of a medical man coming near their wounds – not only are they left to expire in agony, unheeded and shaken off, though catching desperately at the surgeon whenever he makes his rounds through the fetid ship, but now, when they are placed in a spacious building, where we were led to believe that everything was ready which could ease their pain or facilitate their recovery, it is found that the commonest appliances of a workhouse sick-ward are wanting and that the men must die through the medical staff of the British Army having forgotten that old rags are necessary for the dressing of wounds.

*Back on Duty*

William Pearson must have been made of sturdy stuff, for survive he did, though he was eventually certified 'fit for depot duties only'. Despite this he volunteered for service and was to go to India with his regiment where he served throughout the Mutiny. Some thirteen years after joining the 17th Lancers he was discharged from the army and returned to York where he became a turnkey at York Castle Prison. In his later years he lived with relatives in Warmgate, sustained for the last fifteen years of his life by the pension of one shilling a day paid to all Charge of the Light Brigade survivors. On the day he was laid to rest here in his eighty-fourth year, a firing party was provided by the 5th Royal Irish Lancers.

## *James Wilson*

## *York Public Cemetery*

*Life in the Workhouse*

Life inside the Victorian workhouse was intended to be as off-putting as possible. Men, women, children, the infirm, the insane and the able-bodied were housed separately and given very basic and monotonous food such as watery porridge called gruel, or bread and cheese. All inmates had to wear the rough workhouse uniform and sleep in communal dormitories. Supervised baths were given once a week. The able-bodied were given hard work such as stone-breaking or picking apart old ropes called oakum. The elderly and infirm sat around in the day-rooms or sick-wards with little opportunity for visitors, whilst the lunatic paupers lay on boards covered with a coating of loose coconut fibre. Parents were only allowed limited contact with their children – perhaps for an hour or so a week on Sunday afternoon.

*No Charity from the Charity*

Arriving in York in 1853 from Helmsley where he had held a similar position was a new workhouse master – James Wilson, originally from Rievaulx. He arrived with his wife Esther Cole who had also worked at the Helmsley Workhouse as matron: she was to be paid a salary of £20 per year and her husband £40. For the next twenty-six years they jointly ran the workhouse for their employers the Poor Law Guardians, until James' ill health forced their retirement. Their employers spent the next two years discussing a proposal to give them a joint pension of £20 a year, but in the end the Wilsons got nothing more than a testimonial.

*Historical Footnote*

James died in 1882, and his wife Esther in 1895. Some eight years later when their great-grandson, Prime Minister James Harold Wilson KG, OBE, FRC, PC, was seeking a territory appendage for his title on being created a baron, he chose Rievaulx from where his forefathers had originated.